madly chasing peace

madly chasing peace

HOW I WENT FROM Hell TO Happy
IN NINE MINUTES A DAY

dina proctor

NEW YORK

madly chasing peace

HOW I WENT FROM Hell TO Happy
IN NINE MINUTES A DAY

ISBN 978-1-61448-302-1 paperback
ISBN 978-1-61448-303-8 eBook
Library of Congress Control Number: 2012937351

Morgan James Publishing
The Entrepreneurial Publisher
5 Penn Plaza, 23rd Floor, New York City, New York 10001
(212) 655-5470 office • (516) 908-4496 fax
www.MorganJamesPublishing.com

Back Cover Photography by:
Kymberli Quackenbush
www.kymberliqphotography.com

Cover Design by:
Rachel Lopez
www.r2cdesign.com

Interior Design by:
Bonnie Bushman
bonnie@caboodlegraphics.com

In an effort to support local communities, raise awareness and funds, Morgan James Publishing donates a percentage of all book sales for the life of each book to Habitat for Humanity Peninsula and Greater Williamsburg.

Get involved today, visit
www.MorganJamesBuilds.com.

This book is dedicated to anyone
and everyone who has ever wondered,
"is this all there is?!"

table of contents

foreword

by Peggy McColl

Allow me to preface this foreword by telling you about a personal challenge I have.

Many authors send me their books and ask me to read them. So many, in fact, that the stack of books in my office is approaching the size of a small mountain. And, in addition to the physical books authors send me, a virtual pile of e-books is also growing. Authors send them because I specialize in helping them complete their books and/or make them bestsellers. Usually they want my opinion or endorsement, or, in a few rare cases, they ask me to write the foreword for their book.

Now, I do love books; don't get me wrong. But I'd prefer to choose the ones I read, so I usually sigh with dismay when another one lands in my mailbox.

But not when Dina's arrived. When Dina first asked me to read *Madly Chasing Peace*, I was truly excited to do so. I had already met her and been immediately captivated by her authenticity. Dina is a radiant being—loving, giving and profoundly "real"—and I had a strong intuitive feeling that her book would be something special. And frankly, if your book isn't unique in this very crowded marketplace of self-help books, you'll have a tremendous challenge being successful.

So I happily set aside an afternoon to dig into Dina's book, and as soon as I began to read, I was totally captivated. Page by page, I was drawn into her extraordinary story of helplessness and hopelessness and her eventual climb out of that dark place. Dina's book reminded me of one of those page-turning, nail-biting novels that you simply can't put down. And that is precisely what happened. I could not put her book down. As I continued reading, the dinner hour approached and I knew I should set the book aside and prepare a meal for my family. Instead, I ordered in dinner so that I could keep reading!

The book you hold in your hands (or are viewing on your e-reader) is going to do the same for you: grab your attention and not let go until the very last page. It will also inspire you, move you, and give you some powerful yet simple techniques that Dina devised for herself and found to be highly effective. I have tried them and I'm continuing to use them with wonderful results. She calls them "games," and I think it's a good term for them. They are so easy, yet they will awaken an awareness of your inner life that I'll bet you have never experienced before.

At the end of the book, you'll be on the way to finding peace too. And by "peace," Dina means something much more than just the absence of stress. When I first started reading Dina's book, I had the thought, "I'm already peaceful. Peace isn't something I'm seeking." But I found there are life lessons and practices in this book that can take you to a level of self-awareness and fulfillment beyond anything you've aspired to in the past.

It is my sincere wish that you will invest the time to devour every word of *Madly Chasing Peace* and then make full use of Dina's valuable techniques and put her wisdom into practice. And then, for the good of all, I hope you will share this book with those you love and care about and make the world a more peaceful place.

May you stop the madness and be blessed with peace!

"Chaos is only an illusion. It's what
you see when you can't see far enough."
— Deepak Chopra

prologue

I want to want to stop.

I don't *want* to stop; I can't stop. It's the only barrier that I have left to protect me from the world, from my dark emotions, from myself. I am caught in a tornado that I have a vague sense may have been stoppable sometime back but now has me in a full-on downward spiral. I wish I were dead. Every night as I go to sleep, as others say their prayers for health and happiness, my only prayer is that I will not wake up in the morning.

Every morning is excruciating. My body is made of lead; my head is pounding; my skin is itchy; dread permeates my entire being; my anxiety is off the charts. How can I get out of bed and face another day? What is *wrong* with me? There are people out there with real problems—people who are homeless, jobless, crippled…and me, I just can't stop drinking?!

My mind is spinning wildly. *Please, Dina. Get ahold of yourself! You've powered your way through everything in the past until now and it's only made you stronger. You can DO this. Don't let the craving take you. You are tougher than that.*

But in this moment I need relief. The darkness is overwhelming and unbearable. To get out of bed I know I need my secret friend, my drink.

And so the cycle starts one more day.

——

It is Sunday night. I have done many things I thought I would never do over the past few years…slowly selling out to the lure of the high, the secret relief that makes it bearable to get through another day. I cannot forgive myself for too many things to count. Time and again, I have had to drink even when it was most important that I didn't. I'm not an alcoholic; I am a weak, pitiful human being with no self-control, no willpower.

This Saturday I will take my life and leave everyone to their peace. I can see no other way than just to leave this world altogether, to ease the intolerable pain, shame and self-hatred I'm feeling. I am so, so, so sick of myself, my life and everything about everything. I just need a few days to get everything together before I do it. Then, finally, I will be free.

It is early Monday morning. The sun isn't even up yet. I have barely slept. My anxiety and self-loathing have me shaking and sweating. I'm wailing and crying in my apartment alone, thinking of my suicide plan. My orange juice spiked with vodka is the only thing soothing me this morning as I sit on the floor hugging my knees, surrounded by used tissues.

I have no other way out, and the way I'm going now things will only get worse. Maybe some time ago I might have been able to straighten myself out, but I crossed that line a long time back. I can't do this anymore and I don't want anyone to try and help me. I have made my decision. I feel physically sick and kind of crazy. I don't know how I am going to make it through these next six days.

I think about calling a suicide hotline just to speak to someone, but I'd imagine they would try to talk me out of it and that's not what I'm looking for. I really just need a little bit of relief. I have no one in my life who will understand. I can't even bring myself to call Daddy, now sober 17 years. I don't want him to worry, or know the pain I feel, or even think I have a problem with alcohol. I don't want him to be upset or ashamed of me.

Maybe it would make me feel better to see what real drunks are like, to see other people whose drinking is way worse than mine. There is an addiction recovery center up the street. I'll see if they have times when outsiders can sit in on one of their meetings. If I don't like them, if all of their ideas are worthless, at least I'll still have Saturday. Then it will all be over anyway.

I find the number online and call. There's a nightly meeting at 6:00. I ask where to find it. The guy on the phone laughs and says, "You can't miss it; just look for the crowd of people walking in from the parking lot." A crowd of people? I wasn't expecting this. I thought it might be ten people or so. Whatever. It doesn't matter anyway. I'm not going there to make friends. I'm going there to wake myself up and see how bad it could be, to put my own drinking in perspective. I know deep down that I'm not like them. I'm not like anyone at this point.

It's Monday night. I get to the meeting a few minutes early. I feel that weird sensation of being detached, in a dream, walking through a cloud or a fog. I decide that I won't give my real name because my name is kind of unique and what if someone knows my boss or my neighbor's boyfriend or whatever. I have no intention of talking to the people there; I really just want to sit quietly in the back and listen. If anyone asks, I'll just tell them my name is Lisa.

There's a woman outside the door greeting everyone. She smiles, sticks out her hand to me and says, "Welcome, I'm Lisa." I'm completely thrown off that her real name is my fake name, and I give her my real name without thinking. Damn. Oh well. I'll just lay low in the back row and make sure I don't talk to anyone else.

People start coming in, hugging each other, taking seats. There are so *many* of them! I can't believe how many there are. And why are they all happy, smiling, laughing? There is no doubt in my mind that they must have vodka in their travel coffee mugs. If they come to this recovery center, their drinking surely must be way worse than mine, so there's no way they could quit, and there's no way in hell they would be at ease with each other without a drink. In my world there is no possibility of laughter without the warm, protective buzz of alcohol.

This place is weird. Lying, hiding alcohol, and sickly sweet, happy chatter. As soon as it's over, I leave the weird meeting without talking to anyone and drown myself in my usual red wine when I get home.

It's Tuesday night. I barely made it through work today, trying to keep up my happy-la-la-everything's-great facade. I debate inwardly about going to that night's meeting at the recovery center. *Screw it,* I think. *Why go? It will all be over Saturday, anyway.* Besides I have too much wine left over from last night. I'm headed home to find oblivion until I fall into my usual horrifically restless sleep.

It's Wednesday morning. I'm hung over and out of booze. How on earth am I going to make it through the day? On my lunch break, I re-stock and have a couple drinks so I can get rid of this awful headache and nausea. Food matters little. The alcohol puts space around what would normally drive me out of my mind. Everything, especially at work, is much more pleasant and less important when I have alcohol in my system.

On Wednesday evening, I can't bear to go straight home to my depressingly lonely apartment after work, so at the last moment I decide to stop by the meeting at the recovery center. Everyone is warm and friendly, again. It's maddening that they are so damn happy. What is there to be happy about?! I remind myself that it will all be over on Saturday, and I get some comfort from that thought. Just a couple more days of suffering and I'll be done.

At the meeting I happen to sit next to an older guy named Larry who's annoyingly friendly. He asks me if I ever drink in the mornings. I guardedly say, "Maybe." He invites me to meet him tomorrow for an early morning meeting at the center.

"Instead of drinking tomorrow morning," he says, "why don't you meet me here at seven?"

I agree to meet him without really wanting to; I just feel bad that this poor old man is kind of lonely. And I really am a nice person, deep down, so I will help him out. I leave the meeting and get a bottle of wine on the way home.

Generally, I try to buy wine at different times and places so it's not obvious how much I'm buying, but tonight I don't care. I just need it and I need it now. I go to my usual grocery store and pick up one bottle of wine. The line at the checkout is ridiculously long, and the cashier is taking his sweet time, chatting with each customer. Rage boils in me just below the surface. I *need* to get this drink inside of me. I hold myself together on the surface though, and act friendly and casual. *I wonder if anyone here keeps tabs on how much alcohol I buy,* I think to myself.

I never buy more than one bottle at a time for two reasons. One is so I don't look suspicious to anyone who might be noticing what I'm buying, and the other is because only alcoholics ever buy tons of alcohol at a time. I don't do that. I am not one of them.

It's Thursday morning. I wake up restless and horribly hung over. Nothing different from the way I have woken up pretty much every morning for the past couple years. I ransack my brain for what I have left over from last night. Not even enough wine left to take the bite out of this monster headache. Then I remember poor old Larry. He's lonely and will be waiting for me at the stupid center for the meeting. I just do not want to go. But I feel bad for him, so I drag myself out of bed and get dressed. I meet Larry there on time. He immediately introduces me to two women who take my hands and offer me a seat.

Why is everyone being so nice to me? I wonder, a little suspiciously. I can't figure it out. The two women are probably in their 50s and they're dressed professionally; one is wearing a suit. They are so put-together—there's no way these women were ever hard drinkers. I don't want to trust them, but I can't fight the way I feel with them holding my hands.

There is clarity and love in their eyes. Suddenly, I'm at my breaking point. For the first time in my entire life I am completely honest with these women about the extent of my drinking and the depth of my despair. I don't tell them about Saturday. But I cry and cry and cry, and talk and talk and talk. And they listen and hand me tissues.

They promise me that they understand exactly how I'm feeling. They tell me they have been where I am now, and they promise me it gets better. They ask if I plan to go to the meeting here at the recovery center tonight. I wasn't planning on it, but if these nice women will be here tonight, I tell them I promise I'll be here too.

Then they ask, "Do you think you can hold off on drinking just for today, just until you get to the meeting?"

I get the smallest, faintest feeling of hope and a feeling of vague relief that I wasn't expecting. It feels good just not to have the *secret* anymore. I agree to not drink for the next few hours. If I can drink tomorrow then I won't drink today. And they say, "Yes, you only have today. Only make a promise for today."

It's Thursday night. I go to the meeting at the recovery center after work. I have kept my promise. My body feels excruciatingly sick and sweaty and yucky and weak without the usual alcohol in my bloodstream. I am physically shaking. The tears from this morning well up once more, and I cry uncontrollably at the meeting. A couple of women I haven't met before pull me over to sit by them. One is a crotchety old lady. I don't like her. She tells me, "Just don't drink between meetings!"

I think to myself, *Ah ha! That's your brainwashing secret! You tell people not to drink between meetings and then tell them to go to two meetings a day. Well, if I do that forever and ever then I can't ever drink! Screw that. I'm out of here.* I get up and walk out and buy my wine on the way home.

It's Friday morning. I'm at the recovery center again. Those same nice women from yesterday morning hold my hands again and sit next to me and listen to me. They say, "Keep coming back. It gets better."

I let myself hear what they are saying. I look around the room. There are more than 50 people in here and they are *all* alcoholics or addicts of some kind. How on earth did all of them stop drinking?! I can't see it. I don't get it. But on the edge of my mind there is a whisper of an idea that maybe, just *maybe,* there is something I can learn from this room, from these people who have done it.

It's Friday night. I did not drink today. It is torture. I'm in hell and sobbing as I drive home after work. I pull my car into the turning lane to buy my red wine and I cry harder as the liquor store approaches. At the last moment I force myself to pull my car out of the lane and go home instead. Once home I fall onto my bed and I wail and I weep inconsolably for hours. *Am I going to do this thing tomorrow? Am I really going to go through with it?* I tell myself that if those nice women aren't at the recovery meeting in the morning it will be a sign that I should do it; I should get out of here, escape.

I can't tell up from down anymore...and I don't even know if I want those women to be there tomorrow morning or not.

introduction

I've always been spiritually restless. My bookshelves look like a reference library for finding happiness. I have almost every self-help book that ever graced *The New York Times* bestseller list. You need to borrow a book about self-esteem? Hot yoga? Christianity? Atheism? Buddhism? Feng shui? I'm your girl.

If spiritual wisdom wasn't fixing what ailed me at the time, I figured the problem must be nutritional, which is why my shelves also contain books on every healing diet and weight-loss craze, from macrobiotic to raw, from high-protein to vegan, some quietly collecting dust, their spines barely cracked.

My attitude has always been "full throttle or why bother?" I'm a seeker at my innermost core, a spiritual leapfrogger, up for trying anything and everything that might quiet my restlessness and take me a step further on my search for inner peace and true happiness.

And amazingly enough, this crazy quest ended up working out for me...pretty spectacularly, in fact.

My story is about suicidal depression, devastating addiction, a year spent in recovery, and finally, gaining something I'd never had before: deep, lasting, real happiness—complete with experiences of what I can only call a higher state of consciousness. I also moved beyond sobriety and achieved full healing from my alcohol addiction, among other healings in my body and my relationships.

Before I reached this place of peace, I had a lifelong inner ache of emptiness that I tried to fill with many things. Food, men and booze have all taken up an inordinate amount of space in my head and in my life. But I now know that drinking and obsessive dating, radical dieting and all my other self-soothing behaviors were never my problems. They were my solutions, the quick fixes that relieved my inner ache.

So what were my problems? Fundamentally, they all boiled down to one thing: lack of centeredness within myself. Every deep-seated resentment I uncovered was never about the other person; my resentments were always about events that irked me when I was disconnected from my own sense of strength and wellbeing. I wasn't listening to my intuition so I was out of touch with my true nature: the peace, joy and love at my core, which we all originate from. Without that, I got caught up in trying to alleviate ravenous cravings and negative thoughts, when they were merely symptoms of how disconnected I was from my own inner wisdom.

Managing the symptoms alone was like spraying bug repellent on a pile of rotting trash swarming with flies. The bug spray works temporarily, but the flies will just keep coming back until you finally get rid of the trash heap altogether. In my case, the trash heap consisted of all my negative perceptions and self-deprecating thoughts and beliefs. Your trash heap might be different, but for many people I believe our solutions will be the same.

I've written the book in two parts: "My Turn" and "Your Turn." Rather than telling a continuous story, the chapters are self-contained entities. I designed the book this way because I want you to be able to refer back easily to specific stories and practices that resonate with you.

"Part One: My Turn" is a collection of the pivotal times in the last few years when real transformation happened for me. Most chapters contain a story that shows how I learned to handle a situation that used to drive me to drink or binge on food or otherwise react in an unhealthy way. Each of these incidents played a major role in the healing I've experienced, and am still experiencing.

"Part Two: Your Turn" details the techniques (I call them games) that I discovered work for me, plus other games that I developed for those I coach. A few of the games are outlined in the earlier chapters; Part Two provides more explanation. This section serves as a springboard to give you momentum in using the games, whether you follow them step-by-step or give them your own twist.

The amazing thing is, I didn't just overcome alcoholism and depression, I also uncovered my ability to access a higher state of consciousness in the process. In a very short time, I went from being suicidal to being able to see the essence of life all around me and know the truth of life: that we all are radiant beings of light and love, every one of us, whatever disguises we might wear. Having glimpses of this truth and growing more and more solidly established in it, I've been happier and more comfortable in my own skin these past few years than I ever imagined I could be.

Though my breakthrough healing was from addiction, I believe I would have gone through much the same process if I had healed from any chronic illness. My intention behind this book isn't to show how to heal a specific ailment, it's to share the power I found to heal the body by harnessing the mind's power through meditation and intuition.

I don't consider myself to be an expert of any kind, and I don't by any means think that the way I live now is better than any other way of life that works for other people. I'm just a woman who has been to the darkest places inside herself and managed to climb—muddy, thorny branch by cold, rigid stone—back into the warm light of an amazingly happy life, emerging with hope and inspiration to share. These pages detail how I got to where I am today and how I'm currently able to maintain balance and enjoy a more and more profound connection with the beautiful truth of our human existence in my everyday life.

Though I've changed names and details to protect those who would prefer not to be identified, I've done my best to remain true to the crux of my actual experiences.

My hope is that you can take heart from my stories and know that, however dark your path may be right now, you too can shift your perspective, get to know your innermost essence and move steadily from madly chasing peace, to living it more and more fully as each day unfolds.

part one:

my

turn

chapter one

how could this happen to a good girl like me?

"There came a time when the risk to remain tight in the bud was more painful than the risk it took to blossom."
— Anaïs Nin

he agonizing week I described in the Prologue took place in late September 2008. By Friday night of that week I had decided that I just couldn't live with myself any longer. Looking for a sign from God or the universe, I decided that if the two kind women I had met at the recovery center weren't there the next morning, I would end my life with a bottle of my anxiety medication and a bottle of vodka. I thought that should do the job in a not-too-awful way.

So, early that Saturday morning (Suicide Saturday, as I call it), I went to the recovery center for the meeting. I was anxious, sweating and exhausted. I hadn't slept all night.

Hands shaking, I opened the door and walked into the room looking for the two women who had sat with me the past few mornings. There they were, waiting near the door. Their professional weekday attire was replaced with jeans and t-shirts, but the same warmth and compassion was in their eyes. They both grabbed me by the hand right away and led me to a seat.

As much as I willed them not to, my tears came. These poor women had no idea what I'd been planning for later that day. I was relieved that they didn't ask me questions or try to get me to talk. Maybe they sensed that all I wanted was a little comfort from human touch, that I just wanted to sit near them while they held my hands and brushed my tangled, tear-stained hair back from my face.

My body was present in the room, but my mind was a million miles away. My sign had been granted in seeing them, and I thought I would feel relieved. But my desire to escape my inner pain was stronger still than the sign I'd asked for.

Throughout the meeting I couldn't stop myself from continuing to obsess on my suicide plan—the timing, the details, wondering if everything at home and work was organized enough to leave behind. An hour went by too quickly, and the meeting was over. Everyone dispersed. One of the women, Anna, gave me her phone number and told me to call her anytime I needed to talk. Both women hugged me and reminded me that if I kept coming back, things would get better.

I watched them walk out together, feeling detached, like I was in a dream. I had thought that, if I saw them, I would have my answer, but now I wasn't sure. Seeing them had comforted me, but I wasn't convinced that things would get any better if I stuck around longer. My mind was a soupy fog.

I walked out to my car after the meeting but I couldn't bring myself to drive home yet. I couldn't even open the door to my car; I just wasn't ready to head home to die. My anxiety medication and vodka were waiting for me there, ready to send me off to sleep forever. But part of me wasn't ready yet.

I forced myself to take a walk around the block. My mind was spinning with the "should I, shouldn't I?" question and my tears flowed continuously. When I got back to my car I still wasn't ready to get in and drive home, so I took another walk around the same block. My thoughts kept returning to the women at the recovery center. One part of me wanted to see what I could learn from them, even though the other part of me just wanted to end everything.

As I rounded the corner and approached my car for the second time, I suddenly had a thought: I could always just kill myself tomorrow. If I didn't feel right about doing it today, I could just put it off a day. I could do it anytime I wanted to, really. Just not today. Maybe I did want to explore the people at the recovery center more. And if nothing came of it after another day, or two, or three, I'd do it then. It's not like I had to throw out my bottle of pills or anything. I could just keep them safely tucked away until the day came.

That decision ended up saving my life. At the recovery center, lots of people had told me just to focus on today, just to worry about making it through this one day. Of course what they meant was, you don't have to drink today. You can drink tomorrow. Just not today. But what it meant for me was, I don't have to kill myself today. I can always do it tomorrow.

Because one thing was clear: there was no way I was about to quit drinking. I knew I wouldn't be able to keep myself from committing suicide if anyone took away my safety blanket of alcohol. There was no way I could endure life without a drink. I'd much rather be dead than have to feel the excruciating pain of my deep self-hatred and depression. Though my anguish was purely mental, it was as torturous as if the blood in my veins was several degrees warmer than it should be. The constant throb of mental and emotional torment was nearly unbearable.

Of course, I didn't tell anyone that. For weeks I kept going to the center, thinking I'd go to meetings for as long as they'd let me. I was surprised but relieved that they never kicked me out even though I never made a promise to quit drinking.

In between thoughts of suicide and internal debates about whether or not to cut back on my drinking, a nagging question kept arising. I couldn't help but wonder how on earth I could have ended up in this situation. How in the world could a good girl with a privileged Long Island upbringing, who graduated from college with honors just ten years earlier, have ended up this profoundly miserable?

—

My earliest memories are not unhappy ones, but when I compare them to most people's childhood memories, I can see that I took life way too seriously. In my college psychology courses I heard more than one professor say that often people make one or two decisions as children that turn out to be life-determining. Looking back, I know exactly when I made one of those decisions, though of course at the time I had no idea the impact it would have.

I was probably eight years old, sitting in the front passenger seat of the family minivan next to my mom, who was driving. My two younger sisters were in the backseat. As we drove, I looked over and noticed that my mom was crying silently. I was shocked. My mom was a strong superhero, not a person who cried! I got very scared about what might be happening. I remember asking her what was wrong, and she began to cry harder. She pulled over to the side of the road to regain her composure. I was frightened and felt very insecure.

"Mommy, what's wrong?" I asked again nervously, wondering if I'd done something to upset her.

"Oh, Dina, I just don't know what to do!" she sobbed. "What should I do? Please just tell me what to do and I'll do it. I just don't know what to do!"

She kept repeating those words over and over. I know now that she was talking to herself, or maybe to God, but as the oldest daughter, I thought she was talking to me. I thought she needed my help, but I didn't even know what she needed to know how to do.

For my mom, this was a rare five-minute episode in which she lost her composure in front of her kids. For me it was a life-changing moment. I was deeply upset with myself because I thought I should've known what to do, and I didn't. After a few minutes my mom's crying subsided and we continued driving home. But by then, I had made two decisions. I had vowed to myself that (1) I would always know what to do in every situation, and (2) I would do anything I could to make my mom happy. I couldn't bear to see her cry, and I never, ever wanted to be the one who upset her.

This led to my morphing overnight into Super Kid. My parents had always told me how smart I was and how important good grades were. I asked them if they thought I was smart enough to get perfect grades, and they smiled and said, "Of course. You're one of the smartest kids in your class; we can't imagine you would earn anything less than the highest grades in your school."

I believed them and decided I didn't want to just have good grades, I wanted to have the best grades. I wanted to make them the proudest they possibly could be. Looking back today, it's obvious that my well-intentioned idea of demanding perfection of myself led to the chronic anxiety that created the mess I found myself in as an adult. Striving to be impeccable was a curse: if I didn't do everything absolutely perfectly, I wasn't happy.

I had always needed to understand everyone and everything. I remember one time even writing out a questionnaire for my tooth fairy. I asked her if she sold my teeth for money, if I was her only tooth child and if she was invisible. I was curious about these things, but I also needed to know if she was real, so I wanted to compare her handwriting with my parents'. She wrote back that very night and told me her name was Marlene. She neatly printed her response and my parents always wrote in script, so I was able to prove that she existed. Marlene told me that she never sold my teeth, she had lots of other children she visited and she wasn't invisible. She was just very, very small.

As a kid, I also created precise daily schedules for myself, listing when to brush my teeth, do my homework and clean my room. And the times I set weren't 7:00, 7:05, 7:15…those were easy, rounded-off times that anyone could stick to. For my schedule I set times like 7:03, 7:12, 7:19 because only a perfect person could conform to schedules that precise. My deepest need was to be the best I could possibly be, and the closer I kept to my schedule, the better I felt about myself.

Most people wait to have their mid-life crisis until their 40s, but I got mine out of the way the night before my 13th birthday. Of course I planned to live past the age of 26, but the idea of being a teenager, almost a grown-up, terrified me. Most of the grown-ups I knew weren't terribly happy people. My teachers at school were stern and strict, and my parents took life very seriously and always told me how important it was to be responsible. And so far, even with my strenuous self-discipline, I felt that I wasn't good enough, wasn't perfect enough, so I was scared to death that I was going to be a miserable adult. I was afraid I wasn't prepared enough to be a teenager, that much closer to adulthood.

And at 13, I was afraid of getting my period too. That would be the real sign that I was becoming an adult. On my last day of being twelve years old, I felt like some people feel the night before their wedding—being carefree has been fun, having youth and freedom has been a good ride, but now the time has come to settle down. I knew it was all downhill from here, as far as enjoying life was concerned.

And then, a couple of years later when I was in high school, one evening my parents sat me down to talk to me about something important. They told me that my dad had been drinking too much and had started going to a recovery program to get help. He wouldn't be drinking whiskey every night anymore. Well, that was OK with me; that big jug of whiskey in our cupboard smelled terrible and was always in the way when I was trying to get my cereal. It seemed odd though, because I had never seen my dad drunk—or maybe I just didn't know what drunk looked like at that age.

In any case, I made another life-defining promise to myself that night. None of my friends from private school drank, and I'd never tasted alcohol at that point. I vowed that even when I was old enough to drink I would never, ever drink any alcohol whatsoever in front of my dad. And I sure would never get drunk in front of him, whatever "getting drunk" meant.

Later into my teens, as I began comparing myself to my friends, I felt like I was missing something. I had an emptiness inside of me that my friends didn't have. Everyone around me was having fun, and I tried to fit in too, but I never felt like I was one of them, like I was a cool kid that belonged. My ability to maintain straight-A grades and a place in the Honor Society and on the Yearbook Committee didn't enhance my self-esteem. I liked being smart, but it didn't help me feel like I fit in. From the outside no one could tell anything was wrong. But inside, none of my grades or achievements mattered. I saw myself as ugly and different.

My insecurity ran deep, but I never let anyone know that. I worked hard to put on a front of being easy-going and fun, while the black hole inside me continued to expand. I knew no one else felt the same way—everyone else was happy and loving life. I thought something was wrong with me, but I didn't want anyone to think I was weird, so I never told a soul.

Living in the dorms at college, I discovered that my eating habits were different from my friends' too. I saw them have a cookie or two for dessert or a slice of cake at a birthday party and leave it at that. I'd always been sort of a sugar-person. One slice of cake was never enough. I'd eat a cookie or two with other people, then later, alone, I'd finish the box. I always did these mini-binges alone so no one would think I was abnormal.

And it wasn't just food. After watching a TV show or two with my roommate, she'd go off to bed but I'd need to keep going. I'd end up watching hours of mindless shows, sometimes all night long. All-or-nothing was how I lived. A friend of mine once said my mantra was, "If it's good, back the truck up!"

All of my extreme behaviors were an attempt to fill my inner emptiness and make me feel happy. But all the excess food and TV (and later, men and booze) only worked to give me temporary relief. It never lasted because the stuff I was filling this gaping hole with wasn't what I was truly hungry for.

After college, I decided that maybe helping others would give me a sense of purpose and satisfaction. If I could just find something fulfilling to do, I might feel better. Well, true to my all-or-nothing nature, I didn't just volunteer here and there on the side, I found myself on an all-out mission to heal the world, and hopefully myself.

I thought about joining the Peace Corps, but frankly I was scared to live in a third world country, so I found a similar volunteer corps within the U.S. that provided community housing and a small stipend in exchange for my work in a full-time volunteer position. I chose a placement in Southern California, where I'd never been before. I thought changing my environment would fix me, and I didn't just want a new city, I wanted the opposite side of the country.

My volunteer placement was at a homeless shelter for pregnant women. I liked working there but it wasn't as satisfying as I'd hoped, so I started volunteering after-hours as a mentor to teens in juvenile hall. I also tutored kids at a family shelter and helped out on another charity's "bread runs" late at night, picking up that day's leftover bread from nearby bakeries and bringing it to soup kitchens.

Volunteering with yet another organization on the weekends, I made dozens of sandwiches and gallons of soup and brought them to homeless people on skid row in downtown Los Angeles. I met lots of people who called cardboard boxes home, including a guy called Five-Coat Joe. He didn't own a blanket because he learned you could get arrested for sleeping overnight in the park under a blanket, so he used coats instead. He knew all the technicalities of outdoor living.

By the end of that year, I had learned a lot about others whose lives were very different from mine, but nothing had really changed inside of me. If anything, the emptiness had continued to grow. I thought maybe the people I was working with weren't poor enough, and I might find it more satisfying to overcome my fear and go to a third world country and help out. So I took a job working at a non-profit international aid organization and traveled with them to Africa for several weeks. I thought it would be a wake-up call for me to realize how hard others' lives could be, and that might put my life in perspective and launch me into feeling grateful for my life and better about myself.

Well, much to my surprise, the villagers I met in Africa were *happy*. I couldn't believe it! The impoverished women danced joyously and taught me how to swing my hips. (You haven't danced until the village ladies in Africa have swung your hips for you.) Their calm, wide-eyed children were curious and affectionate, constantly smiling and patting my long, fine brown hair and soft, pale, sun-protected skin. I was more confused than ever. What on earth had these folks—who lived without running water and electricity—figured out that I hadn't?! How could they possibly be so much happier than I was? They were so poor! And yet I felt they were giving me more than I was giving them.

I worked for non-profits for several years and was even honored with the U.S. President's Volunteer Service Award two years in a row for my volunteer work. And yet, I still felt unfulfilled. In fact, I felt horribly empty inside. And so, when the position I was holding lost its funding, I felt it was time to try something else. I went to a temporary employment agency to find work, and they placed me in a paid administrative job. I still volunteered in my free time, doing office work and raising money for an organization that brought clothing and computers to South America.

Time passed and as I got further into my twenties, I found myself swinging in and out of a growing depression. I saw ads on TV asking, "Are you lonely? Does it feel like no one understands you? Is it a struggle just to get out of bed in the morning?" and my answers were always: yes, yes, YES! That's ME!

So I called a number from an ad for a depression research study and made an appointment. The female doctor I met with diagnosed me with Major Depressive Disorder. She put me on various anti-depressant medications but none worked; they just made me extremely sleepy. I liked the attention I got in the study, but at the same time I felt like no one there really understood exactly how I was feeling. They asked all the right questions, but I could tell they had never been depressed themselves. And I felt like they thought I was weird and abnormal. I quit the study feeling even more alone.

After that I tried talk therapy and even joined a depression support group, where we all commiserated together. One man in the group had post-traumatic stress from a dog bite he had suffered during his job as a construction worker. He had such severe depression and anxiety that he couldn't return to work. Another had survived a suicide attempt. Boy, that had to suck. The depression group was only making me more depressed.

The sessions with my one-on-one therapist were pleasant enough, but I could tell she had never felt the way I did. She gave me little homework assignments, like washing the dishes, which I could barely muster up the energy to do. It took so much out of me to act happy at work and with my friends that all I wanted to do when I was alone was lie on my couch and watch TV. Dishes and dust bunnies piled up.

Months went by and nothing was working. I began to think that if nothing was going to change and I was never going to be happy, I'd rather just be dead. If life was going to suck this badly, if therapy and medications weren't going to work, then why bother? I found myself crying almost every night.

I felt like I had tried everything: I had changed jobs several times, changed boyfriends, moved across the country. I had even changed my name, adding Proctor (my Grammy's maiden name) as my last name after my Grammy passed away. I had been very close to her, and she was always such a happy person. I thought changing my name might help me recreate my identity and give me a fresh start as a new and hopefully happier person, like she was. But no matter how many times I tried to reinvent myself, nothing worked. Desperation had me hanging by a thread.

In my late twenties I had the idea that living by myself might be contributing to my melancholy nature, and living with other people might give me a breath of fresh air. I decided to move in with two guys in my group of friends who were looking for a roommate to share their three-bedroom house. At first it helped immensely to have other people around to distract me from my negative thoughts. I actually stopped wishing I were dead for awhile.

Up until living with them, I had never been a party-girl. During my college years, yes, I'd gotten drunk on weekends with my friends, but throughout my twenties I hadn't drunk much alcohol at all. But these guys liked to drink a beer or two every night after work, so I got into the habit too. I also met some new women friends who liked to go out and party. After a while, a small group of us girls were going out six nights a week. I'd never done anything in moderation, and my party lifestyle became no exception.

I re-discovered the excitement of dating as I partied more and more. I thought that if I could just find the "one," my future husband, I would finally find my happiness. I joined every Internet dating site I heard about, and over a span of six months, I met 86 guys—in person! I figured that if I left no stone unturned and just met *everyone*, at some point Mr. Wonderful would have to end up sitting across from me. Sometimes I planned nights of triple-headers, meeting one guy at 5:00, one at 7:00, and one at 9:00. Frustratingly, though, none of these men ended up being my soul mate.

Another new discovery in my party phase was the magic of alcohol. My girlfriends and I made it a game to see how many free drinks we could get from guys at the bars every night. Half the time we didn't even bring cash with us, knowing that if we flirted the right way all the drinks we wanted would be free. We got into the habit of "pre-partying," having a drink or two together before we hit the nightclub scene. It didn't take too many nights out for me to realize that having a drink in me before even leaving the house gave me the confidence I'd never had before, which really helped me enjoy meeting new people, especially guys.

After a couple of months of nightly partying, I became uncomfortable going out at all without a pre-party drink. Booze became the magic fairy dust that made everyone cuter and friendlier, including myself. My favorite line with a guy who offered to buy me a drink was, "Are you sure you want to do that? I'm an expensive date. It's a two-drink minimum and I only drink martinis." No one ever turned me down. For the first time in my life, my confidence was soaring.

But the high didn't last. After about a year of the party lifestyle I started to get kind of sick of the nightly pattern. The story was always the same, and I was getting bored with the five-step routine my friends and I had fallen into: (1) drink, (2) go out and drink more, (3) meet lots of guys, (4) get home, fall into bed and pass out, (5) wake up four hours later, hung over, and have to go to work. I was just tired of it and wanted to start a calmer lifestyle, so I found a new place to live with a new roommate who wasn't a partier. It was a good change, but I was so in the habit of having a couple of drinks after work that I continued that ritual in my new digs. My roommate didn't mind though. She had no idea I had crossed an invisible line into alcohol dependency, and at that time, neither did I.

By this point I was approaching 30. I had more alone time since I wasn't going out much anymore, and that led to my slipping in and out of depression once again. I was about to be 30 and unmarried. What better reason to feel sorry for myself? Without my party ritual, I had a lot of quiet time in the evenings to think. It occurred to me that perhaps what I needed to do was seek within. Maybe pick up a spirituality practice, go learn to meditate or join a yoga class or something. So I went to the local bookstore and picked out some spiritually enlightening books.

Home in the evenings, I would drink my usual wine and settle in for some reflection time. I read books by Eckhart Tolle and the Dalai Lama. Surely their peaceful souls had some helpful hints for me. Strangely enough, though, I couldn't really understand what these books were saying. The words kind of sounded like "blah blah blah" to me.

A friend once told me that he liked to read spiritual books when he was high on marijuana because they made so much more sense. I thought maybe that would work for me too. Perhaps being in a higher state would make all this spiritual stuff fall into place. (Praying and fasting my way to enlightenment just wasn't for me.) So I got some marijuana from friends who also took the time to teach me how to inhale it. I drank my wine and smoked a little pot alone at night while reading my new books. I had my brand new notebook handy to record any revelations that might whisper to me in this mellow, high place. More often than not, though, the notebook pages remained empty and I ended up passing out in my own drool; I never got the booze/weed quotient precise enough to make any real progress.

At this point I felt the depression creeping back and I was desperate to fend it off. I thought that maybe fasting was the way to go after all. I'd never actually been overweight, but my self-image definitely was, and over the years, I had tried every diet I could find. I'd been on high-protein diets, eating hot dogs for breakfast because they were a lot easier to cook than bacon and eggs, and I'd gone completely vegan, eating only brown rice and broccoli for days on end. But, despite all my dieting efforts over the years, my self-image had just gotten worse. With this new commitment to finding spiritual enlightenment, or even just some fleeting moments of peace, I began to try drastic juice cleanses and days of eating only raw vegetables. I thought maybe if I cleared all the toxins from my body I would feel better about myself. About everything, really.

Well, guess what? It didn't work. The only thing that was working at this point was booze. Alcohol gave me space around my negative thoughts and took the focus off my self-loathing and depression.

I thought about trying anti-depressant medications again. Maybe medical science had developed something new over the last few years that would cure me. But I talked myself out of it, rationalizing that alcohol was a much more natural solution. After all, wine is made from grapes. Pills are just chemicals.

By the time I hit 32 I had gradually slipped all the way back into the clutches of my old demon, clinically known as Major Depressive Disorder. My nightly drinking had progressively turned into around-the-clock drinking. Every morning I'd have spiked orange juice for breakfast, just to take the edge off my monstrous alcohol-withdrawal headache. By lunchtime the hangover would be back and I'd need a couple of drinks to make it through the afternoon. Nighttime, of course, was my usual red wine. I never considered cutting back on my drinking because it was the only thing that soothed me and gave me relief. I was past the point of looking for a good buzz with alcohol; I was just trying to ward off the horrible withdrawal symptoms that came with lack of alcohol in my bloodstream.

And so we come to my lowest point: the summer of 2008. A few months earlier I had taken a new job in Santa Monica and moved into a place by myself. I'd needed (yet another) change and thought a fresh start with new people and a new city might shake me out of this depression and boozing cycle. Well, I think you know what happened—I changed locations but took myself with me. Emotional agony consumed me.

Every ounce of my effort went into managing my alcohol consumption so none of my friends or co-workers would know the extent of my drinking. It was only with alcohol coursing through my veins that I could even pretend to be happy. I started having vivid thoughts of suicide once again. I didn't have anyone I could talk to. I felt—as I had many times over the last several years—like I was weird and abnormal, and I didn't want any of my friends or my family to know what a mess I was inside. So I faked it by day and drowned myself in wine by night.

September 2008 was my little sister's wedding back on Long Island. I was so flattered to be the maid of honor, but at the same time I felt disproportionately overwhelmed by my event-planning and toast-making responsibilities. As the date approached, I became completely mired in my swamp of misery and depression. I knew I wouldn't be able to make it through the wedding events without drinking, but foremost in my mind was my promise to myself half a lifetime ago that I would never, ever drink in front of my dad.

When the day finally arrived, I put all of my willpower into trying to resist having a drink at the reception. Sadly, I failed. Booze was flowing freely and I couldn't help myself. I drank quite a lot and got very drunk. Since drunk people aren't unusual at a wedding, no one thought anything of my drinking, even my dad. But I knew.

I couldn't avoid knowing that I'd broken my lifelong promise, and I couldn't bear the shame I felt. I had crossed the line I'd been dancing around the past several months; I had finally reached the tipping point where I simply could not live with myself any longer. Suicide had been an appealing fantasy up until that point, but after breaking my lifelong vow to myself, I felt I had no choice but to go through with taking my life. I had finally hit rock bottom.

The week following the wedding was the week I started going to meetings at the recovery center and putting one day at a time between Suicide Saturday and the present moment. The only comfort I got was from telling myself I could always kill myself tomorrow. Knowing I could hover near the "game over" button gave me a warped sense of relief and just enough resolve to stay alive one day longer.

But warding off suicide one day at a time is no way to live.

chapter two

surrender

"If you want something you've never had before, you need to do something you've never done before."
— Drina Reed

hey say when you hit rock bottom, there's nowhere to go but up. Well, in my experience that's not true. The bottom floor that I'd slammed down onto had a trap door.

After a couple of weeks of going to meetings at the recovery center one slow, torturous day at a time, I began to realize that just going to these meetings every day and actually doing the work of getting sober are two different things entirely. I still didn't talk much to anyone there, but I accepted hugs when they were offered. The thing was, I had no intention of quitting drinking. I just wanted to be able to go to this safe place, this safe space where I could sit with nice women who held my hands and let me cry. But I still didn't really believe I was one of them.

Once a week at the meetings they gave out little coins to congratulate people on staying sober for 30, 60, 90 days, or whatever. I didn't understand why these people had to quit entirely. Why didn't they just get some self-control? That was my plan. This 30-day idea was the perfect test for me. I could use their little game to prove to them (and to myself) that quitting altogether is really not necessary, that it's kind of an overkill solution, actually. Besides, the coins were for 30 days of "sobriety" and that just meant being "not drunk," right? So I figured I would let myself drink socially, by which I meant I could have a glass of wine at dinners and parties with two rules: (1) I wouldn't let myself drink enough to get buzzed, and (2) I forbade myself to drink alone. I reasoned that if I could pull that off for a whole month, it would prove that I was over this out-of-control drinking phase.

Shortly after I committed to my 30-day resolution, I was invited to a good friend's wine tasting party. I'd never been much into wine tasting—I've always been more into wine *drinking*—but I was sure I'd be fine just sipping. Besides, it would be nice not to have to worry about driving drunk afterwards. I was excited to get to the party and test out my new theory.

When I arrived at the party that Saturday night, instead of going straight to the bar area as I normally would have, I disciplined myself to wait until a glass of wine was offered to me. I hadn't had a drink since I'd started my little challenge a week earlier, and I was more than happy to accept a beautiful half-filled glass of red wine when it was offered. I took a small sip, just letting a taste touch my lips, and a warm sensation enveloped my body. It wasn't even having the wine in my system, it was the promise of it in that first taste that gave me the all-is-well feeling. I held my glass and scanned the room, watching every single person and how they handled their wine.

Some people were drinking heavily, the way I had gotten used to doing, but most were just happily chatting, with the wine seeming to be more of an afterthought. I only half-participated in conversations because my mind was so preoccupied with noticing how everyone else was drinking their wine, and rationalizing in my mind whether I could have another half-glass yet. My thoughts were all about how much to let myself drink, how much my friends were drinking, and a growing tinge of self-pity that I couldn't just relax and drink like I wanted to. I kept telling myself that if I could just stop thinking about drinking so much I'd be OK.

When I finally finished my first half-filled wine glass, I felt a compelling physical craving for more wine. Reminding myself that I was still in my 30-day trial period was the only thing that kept me from drinking more. I knew that if I could just make it 30 days I would have proven I wasn't an alcoholic and I wouldn't have to go through the program at the recovery center after all. My body screamed in craving and the voice in my head screamed back, *Dina, you're overreacting! Just calm down and stop thinking so much about the damn wine!* But I just couldn't enjoy myself. My wine obsession was taking up too much of my energy. I left the party early and drove home, stone cold sober.

For 30 entire days, I continued just like that. I sipped wine only at parties or while having dinners with friends. I didn't even catch a buzz that whole time! I was so proud of myself. *See?* I thought. *I did it. I proved I didn't have an alcohol problem! All I'd needed was some time away from it to regain perspective!* Everything was fine. I went to the recovery center and proudly accepted my 30-day coin. Everyone congratulated me. I felt great and they didn't even know why. It was because I wasn't one of them. Anyone who could ingest alcohol and stop themselves with sheer willpower before getting a buzz would never be categorized an alcoholic.

So that was me. The Normal Drinker.

And then I got drunk.

I invited some girlfriends over for brunch the Saturday morning after my 30-day success. Not a single one of them knew I was going to this recovery center. None of them knew that I'd almost committed suicide. I hadn't confided in anyone. I was too afraid that they would think badly of me or see me as weak, or lose respect for me if they knew what had been going on with me for the past couple of months. I'd always been good about keeping up my happy-la-la-everything's-great facade when I'd seen them. So this brunch was just supposed to be a fun little get-together of girlie giggles and gossip.

One of my friends brought over a bottle of champagne to splash into our juice. A couple of people took a little bit for their orange or cranberry juice, but I declined. So proud of myself. Then, after everyone had left my place and I was cleaning up, I saw that the champagne bottle was still almost full.

I was alone. Just me and the booze. The voice in my head piped up. *That's a perfectly good (expensive!) bottle of champagne! You'd be crazy to pour it down the sink!* Plus, of course you can't re-cork champagne. You pretty much have to use it or lose it.

I decided that I could let myself drink it if I drank it super slowly and didn't let myself catch a buzz.

But once my first half-glass went down so smoothly and I started to feel the familiar, wonderful warmth wash through me, the sleeping tiger of craving woke up inside of me. Alone at home with the champagne, without planning to, I finished the bottle. The tiger began raging. I had no choice. It commanded my body to walk down the street to the grocery store to get some wine. The tiger was now ravenous and vicious, demanding to be fed.

I spent the rest of the weekend alone at home. Drinking. Passing out. Waking up. Drinking. Passing out. Over and over. I tried to watch movies to distract myself from the all-too-familiar shame and self-hatred I felt. I wanted more than anything to talk to someone, but I had no one I could call. All the recovery center people would be so disappointed in me and there was no way I could tell my friends or family about this.

Desperation and bleak misery pulled me once again into their dark cloud, and I began to debate with myself again about taking my bottle of pills. Obsessive thoughts of suicide ravaged me once more. Then, suddenly I realized with horror that I had been so stupid! I'd admitted my suicide plan to some new friends at the recovery center. If I ended up dead now, it wouldn't look like an accidental overdose—everyone would know I had killed myself. And I couldn't bear to do that to my family.

I thought my agony the week that I had first planned my suicide was the lowest that a human being could feel. I learned on Champagne Weekend that deeper pits of emotional despair and mental anguish and self-hatred did, in fact, exist. Controlling my drinking was the only thing in my life that, despite exerting 110% of my willpower, I couldn't control. I couldn't believe I couldn't do it. But I couldn't.

I returned to the recovery center meeting on Monday morning, crying once again. I didn't want to go there, but I had nowhere else to go. I spilled the truth to my new friends and no one was mad at me. No one was ashamed of me. In fact, many people told me they had done the same thing at one time.

At long last, I turned my will over to the group. I didn't even have my "game over" button anymore, with the option of suicide being off the table. The jig was up. It was time for me to do as they told me.

And who would have guessed? Sometimes surrendering is the first step to winning the battle.

chapter three

reinventing God

"As far as inner transformation is concerned, there is nothing you can do about it. You cannot transform yourself, and you certainly cannot transform your partner or anybody else. All you can do is create a space for transformation to happen, for grace and love to enter."

— Eckhart Tolle

wo things became very clear to me after I committed to joining the recovery center's program (and to giving up drinking altogether). I was told I needed to choose a coach to guide me individually through the recovery program, and I needed to believe in God. Everyone in the program talked about God all the time: how God had taken away their obsessive need to drink, how God had saved them from themselves, how God had transformed their lives.

All this magical God talk, which I didn't really believe in, really turned me off.

Fortunately, my new coach, a woman named Grace, didn't demand that I believe in the God I had grown up with. In fact, she insisted that I find my own idea of God, one that worked for me. Grace told me that the important thing was to rely on a higher power instead of relying on my self-will, as I'd done so far in my life.

"Start praying and start meditating," were Grace's first instructions to me.

I had chosen Grace as my coach because she was a couple of years older than I was, in her mid-thirties, and so put-together, so comfortable in her own skin, that I was immediately drawn to her. She talked about her drug and alcohol addiction very openly and had a feeling of lightness and freedom about her. I liked being around her and I inherently trusted her.

Part of the prayer and meditation homework Grace gave me was to become willing to set aside everything I thought I knew, so I could have an open mind for a new experience. Upon hearing that suggestion, I balked immediately.

"Set aside everything I *think* I know?! What does that mean?! I do, in fact, *know* that I know what I know!" I exclaimed hotly.

Grace smiled at the fire behind my objection. "I'm not telling you to disregard everything you've ever learned, but if you want to be successful in this program, you need to be willing to live your life in a different way. To think about things differently. I'm not asking you to *give up* everything you know, just to set it all to the side for the moment, so you can create some space inside yourself for new ideas to take root. And after you've gone through this program, if you don't find you like these new ideas, you can have your old way of thinking and living back exactly as it is today."

Her calmness at my objection took me by surprise. I was curious as to how she could be so confident in what she was instructing me to do. Her confidence, her openness and her comfort with herself really hooked me. I wanted what she had.

Then Grace said, "Besides, look at where your best thinking has gotten you so far."

She said it matter-of-factly, knowing all too well my story of the last couple of months.

That comment stopped me cold. I began to consider what she was saying. *Maybe she's got a point,* I told myself. *I can give her ideas a try for a few weeks or a month, and I can always bail out.* Reluctantly (and mostly because I didn't have any better ideas), I agreed to follow her instructions.

As part of the meditation practice she was starting me on, Grace told me to sit quietly and focus on nothing but my breathing for 20 minutes every morning. Though this didn't seem like it would do much of anything, I didn't have any other promising solutions. I agreed I would try it out.

I'd never been a meditator, had never really done it successfully or consistently, but it was something I'd always wanted to be good at. I just never could find that inner place of peace, even though I'd wanted it more than anything for as long as I could remember. My past experiences with meditation had always been like my New Year's resolutions to work out regularly at the gym. I'd made half-hearted attempts, given up before seeing any results, and comforted myself with, "I'll try again tomorrow." The problem was that "tomorrow" always brought guilt about yesterday's failure. Defeated, I concluded time and again that maybe I just wasn't made for it after all. Whenever I tried to sit still, my negative thoughts ate me alive like ravenous mosquitoes on a humid summer evening.

At this point, mere weeks were separating me from the lowest time in my life, and holding myself back from taking a drink was still a moment-to-moment stress. I was in a constant state of nervous energy, what I call "idling high." Despite my commitment to trying it, I couldn't fathom how I could possibly sit still and be with myself, undistracted, for 20 whole minutes. I avoided it for days, until finally I took it on as a challenge to overcome. *It's got to work if I just commit to keeping at it*, I reasoned. Wise sages from around the world find true salvation in meditation. Maybe it could work for suicidal alcoholics too.

After several times of trying to meditate as Grace instructed, I realized that although I couldn't make it for 20 minutes without feeling like I would crawl out of my skin, I was able to sit relatively still and focus on my breathing for three minutes. I thought Grace would be mad when I told her this, but instead she was encouraging.

"Whatever you can do is great, Dina. Just keep it consistent."

By the time six weeks had passed, I'd settled into a comfortable routine of sitting and trying to focus on my breath for just three minutes, three or four times a day. Nothing much seemed to happen during these mini-meditations, but I didn't mind them either. This was progress, since even three minutes alone with my thoughts, temptations and inner demons had seemed unthinkable only weeks before.

A few more weeks went by. And then, at home one afternoon in February 2009, I picked up my copy of Eckhart Tolle's *The Power of Now* with renewed curiosity. I'd heard so much about this book from friends and wanted so badly to be able to grasp its message. Reading it all the way through was something I'd been trying to accomplish for the last few years. But I'd always felt that the message was just outside of my grasp; frustratingly, I just could not get to a place of comprehending the concepts and ideas there. Instead of getting enlightenment or inspiration from the book, all I ever got was a monster headache and a caffeine craving.

I knew from my friends who had read the book that its message is spiritual and powerful, its core idea reminding us that simply being present in the current moment is the key to happiness. This sounded simple enough to read and grasp, though way too simple to be the key to happiness. I had very rarely been focused in the moment I happened to be in; my mind was always worried about something I had messed up yesterday or what I was going to screw up tomorrow. I had never been good at "right now."

But this time around, something was different. Maybe thanks to my daily mini-meditations, I had a surprising ability to focus on the words and the message, and I could see why people were excited about it. I began to open up to the idea that nothing in the circumstances of my life needed to change. For the first time I had a sense, a knowing, that my discontent and depression were not due to anything outside of myself. The only thing that needed to change was my ability to focus my binoculars on my own life. And that, I discovered, begins with being fully present in the moment that I'm currently in.

After reading and absorbing the gist of the book over several days, one of my meditations was different than usual. This is how I wrote about it in my journal at the time:

The couch in my apartment is where I usually meditate, and that is where I am sitting now, just opening my eyes after my three minutes of silence. I look around, moving my head very slowly. The room feels profoundly quiet. My cat, KC, is sitting next to me, and I am gazing at him with a depth of love and warmth I've never felt before. Time is moving at an exaggeratedly slow pace. I don't have a single thought in my head. Not only is the apartment silent, my mind is silent. Usually when I look at my cat, I reach out and pet him and talk to him conversationally as if he could understand me. In this moment, though, the silence is so compelling that the desire to talk to him doesn't even arise.

Something inside my body is relaxing, opening. I look again, very, very slowly, around the room. My eye catches the thin coating of dust dancing on the wood floor, illuminated in a sunbeam. The floor looks exceptionally beautiful, every scratch and mark contributing artfully to the character of the perfect, well-worn wooden boards. The wooden chest on the opposing wall takes my breath away. Has it always been so striking?!

I look again, moving my head very slowly, over at KC. His eyes meet mine. My mind is still silent; there are no words in my head. I'm not sure if this has ever happened before. KC and I are exchanging affection through our gaze alone. I do a double-take when I realize that he's communicating with me—not in words, of course, but through his eyes, his gaze, just the energy of his little being. It's ridiculously obvious and no big deal. It's just what he always does, how he's always been. How had I never picked up on this before? A calm and steady, gentle and deeply loving energy is unquestionably radiating from him to me. I can feel it so clearly that I can almost see it. In a corner of my mind a familiar fear stirs, the fear of losing him. Stronger than that fear, though, is that steady wave of energy from him to me. Within a moment or two, the fear subsides.

I stumble upon a knowing, an awareness, that all is well, all is always well, and that all will still be well when KC transitions out of my life. I have never felt so at peace with the notion of death. There's a bottomless stillness inside me, and for the first time I'm seeing life from a refreshing new viewpoint: There is nothing wrong with death; the circle of life with all its joys and anguishes is really an OK thing. It's like I'm being let in on the bigger picture, a broader perspective on life.

I went about my life as usual over the next few days. But my mind remained silent. There were no words in my head for about three days. And I had a compelling inclination to move very, very slowly in everything I did. Have you ever had the experience of feeling like time was moving in slow motion when you were falling or otherwise in a dangerous or critical situation? It was like that, except without any fear or urgency. I wonder if it's because when you're falling you become ultra-present in the moment, so your perspective of time changes and your mind chatter stops temporarily. Whatever the reason, it's the closest analogy to explain how exactly I felt. Again, I wrote about my experience:

> I'm noticing everything. Tiny wrinkles in the shower curtain; the way the sun glints across the glass table; each jagged rock in the sidewalk pavement; feelings and sensations. Brushing my teeth feels like a massage! It is unbelievably sensual and pleasurable. Have my senses always been dulled by some kind of protective coating? Have I been numb my entire life?
>
> My three-minute meditations are extraordinarily satisfying. My ability to focus is unencumbered; anything I put my attention on takes up the focus of my entire self. And my eyes are seeing the world from an odd perspective: my head, my eyes, and my consciousness all feel like they are above my body! I am fully present in the moment but feel much bigger than my physical self. My awareness is floating above, but still tethered to, my body. There is a Big Me observing the body of Little Me. This lasts as I go about my day. I watch myself in conversation with others and see Big Me looking at Little Me

with such affection and love. I see myself telling a funny story and realize that many of the conversations I have don't really mean anything. Little Me is on auto-pilot, chattering away, while Big Me knows that not nearly as many words are needed as Little Me uses constantly.

During these three days, I also feel "high." It isn't the most pleasant sensation, though that might be just because it is so unfamiliar. I am hyper-aware of everything my eyes absorb and my fingers touch. My senses are ultra-sensitive. It is the most alive I have ever felt, but it's overwhelming, almost like I'm not quite ready for it.

I feel like I'm being let in on the secret of how the world really is, how life operates at the core. What's totally amazing is realizing that my body (the Little Me) is only about five percent of who I am, that all physical bodies are just finger puppets that the Big Me within animates. It's ridiculously obvious to me—so obvious that I can't believe I never saw this before—that my body and what I observe with my five senses are nothing but a barometer of how freely I allow Big Me to direct Little Me. It's like the physical world is just a symptom of how connected I am to the other 95% of who I really am. I have a knowing deep in my bones that if I want to cure or change or heal anything about my body or my physical experience, all I need to do is relax, trust and fully believe in Big Me's nudges, which are the inklings of my intuition.

It's equally obvious that pure joy and happiness aren't hard to attain, they are actually my most natural state, the most natural state of all living beings, and any experience other than pure joy can be turned around quickly if I release all resistance to my present circumstances and allow Big Me to run every aspect of the show. But I'm also aware that before now I'd never even known that Big Me (which is 95% of who I am!) even existed, and I'm quite sure no one else around me knows that either.

What's also so clear to me right now is that my normal way of living—using logic, reason and willpower—is the hard way to go about it. I don't know anyone who doesn't live this way, and yet, in this expanded state I'm in, I know that I've completely blown right past the state of consciousness where logic and reason dominate. Logic and reason are a step along the way of life and learning but are definitely not the ultimate perspective to live from.

These feelings gradually dissipated and the chattering voice in my head started up again. I was back to "normal" after three days (whatever "normal" is for two months sober) and life went on. Though *The Power of Now* doesn't describe an experience with the Big and Little Me, I'm sure that the essence of what I felt—being fully present and completely free of thoughts of the past and future—are what Eckhart Tolle is describing. The weekend was unforgettable, and I wondered if this experience would ever happen to me again. Was my little meditation practice slowly removing the anesthetic from all my nerve endings, and from my heart? Would everything feel this significant going forward?

Now, as I reflected on Grace's instruction to rely on God, not my self-will, I thought about this experience a great deal. In those three days it had become obvious to me that a state of higher consciousness, previously a mystery to me, was not propaganda, but actually real. I could accept that possibility, but a God that I could contact and connect with was harder to believe in. It was something I hadn't thought about in a long, long time. And even when I had thought about it, as a child in parochial school, I hadn't had the life experience to realize why it even mattered.

My childhood God was a super-busy, all-powerful being I felt I shouldn't bug too much because He had a lot to do, helping people who had much bigger problems than I did. I never wanted to hog all of God's attention because I didn't want to take anything from those who needed Him more. Who wants to lob in a request for a good SAT score when someone else has a call in about civil war or a sick baby? Besides, the values my parents instilled in me were that "hard work is virtuous" and "it's up to me to make things happen in my life." I was strong enough and smart enough to succeed without needing to wimp out and call in outside help, not from my friends or parents, and certainly not from God, who was busy helping people who really needed it.

For the past ten years or so, I had called myself an atheist-by-default. I did my time, 18 solid years, in Catholic school. But after I left religious education, it just started to make more sense that there was no God rather than there was a God, largely because of all my experiences with poor people. As a child, I had always thought that God blessed good people throughout their lives and damned bad people throughout theirs. But how could a loving God not take care of the wonderful yet impoverished people I'd met in my volunteer work? What had they done to deserve their difficult, penniless lives? It just didn't make sense that the kind and virtuous poor people I'd met were being punished. There must be something else at work that would explain their poverty. I didn't see them being mistreated by God, but I sure didn't see them being saved either. Atheism had just started to make more sense.

So I'd made my own peace about God, and really it came down to a simple observation: I had never seen anything outside of creation that did not exist within it. It seemed that the source and energy of life was contained within the beings of the world, not held by an exterior entity running a puppet show.

Seen in this light, Grace's insistence that I rely entirely on God for my life direction seemed completely impractical. My self-will had gotten me everywhere until now. Wasn't that a good thing? Wouldn't it be better for me and for everyone else if I took responsibility for my own life and success? Everything I'd accomplished—my straight-A grades, my college scholarship, to say nothing of all my jobs and boyfriends—wasn't up to God: I did all that work! Everything that I had in life—my job, my money, my car, my apartment—was a direct result of my sweat, tears, effort and planning. I was proud of my accomplishments and proud that I had never relied on any outside power, even another person, for my success. Asking God to help me with these things would have been the wimpy way out. The God I knew rewarded hard work! "God helps those who help themselves"...right?

But after my experience of those three days of inner silence, a new idea made its way into the back of my mind. I'd had a glimpse of a remarkable energy, a power source that is abundant and readily available to all. I definitely did not get the impression that my access to it was in any way robbing some other needy soul of their chance to feel that way too. I began to think there was a perspective on God that I couldn't quite grasp yet, but that would make sense to me eventually. I just couldn't quite put my finger on what it was.

I decided to write about all of this in my journal. Sometimes the process of writing opens up and clarifies a new idea for me. I began writing about the difference between the sheer willpower and brain power I've always relied on to get everything done versus the ease of connection I had felt over those three days. My new energy had felt effortless—like all I had to do was "let" life happen versus "make" life happen.

My writing led me to reflect on old mythological ideas of gods and how God has been thought of throughout history. I also thought of the walks I'd been taking in the sun as often as possible just to get out of my lonely apartment. As I remembered the wonderful feeling of the sun warming my face and the tops of my shoulders, the image of an ancient sun-god popped into my mind. I wondered, *What about the sun had made people at one time consider it a god? Well, it's definitely a power greater than any human, and it's something people wouldn't be able to live without. In fact, Earth as we know it couldn't exist without the sun.*

Ideas and words began to pour through me onto my journal pages. I felt this sun-god analogy might lead me somewhere. I kept writing.

I couldn't imagine that the sun had had a grand scheme to fulfill such a daunting, important role, keeping an enormous system of planets in balance. It's just going about its thing, just being the sun. Yet all life exists because of it. Flowers along the sidewalk aim their little blooming faces in the direction of the sun, searching for and getting the nourishment they need. And I would guess that the sun isn't feeling diminished by giving these flowers what they're seeking. The sun feels warm and wonderful on my face during my walks too. It's providing this great service to all forms of life without even knowing or intending it, as far as I can tell.

One thought led to another as I continued to scribble furiously. Sunshine is abundant and it doesn't discriminate. It remains steady and strong no matter how many people, animals and plants tap into its energy. The sun isn't choosing who or what might benefit from its light and heat. I can choose to bask in the sun, to thrive and be in the light, or I can choose to hole up inside, draw the shades and banish myself from the sun. If I spend day after day lying on the beach, absorbing as much sun as I want, I'm not hogging its attention or energy, nor am I taking the opportunity to absorb sunshine away from anyone else, no matter how much time I spend outside.

My train of thought led to a little breakthrough. The sun provides energy for growth and does not intentionally punish or kill any living beings who choose to cut themselves off from it. As I child I'd believed that if someone was killed or injured or poor, it was because God was punishing them. Over time, this was one of the ideas that had turned me away from my childhood God. It just didn't make sense to me that God would be that cruel.

Now, some would say that nature (or God) is, in fact, cruel, and in viewing animals devouring each other in the wild, or the aftermath of hurricanes and tidal waves, I can see why people could think that. But ever since I reached adulthood, I've had a core belief that there is no moral judgment connected with any of these things. How could there be, if that is the natural order of life? These events just are what they are. Animals and people aren't judged and then punished by pain and suffering; life and death are just happening. Time is just marching on.

My thoughts flashed back vividly to my experience of accepting KC's mortality during my three days of inner silence. At that time I knew there was nothing punishing about death. There's no grim reaper looking for fresh victims; there's no dark sun that emanates blackness, creating nighttime here while the golden sun is busy illuminating the other side of the earth. There is no source of darkness, no source of evil. Darkness is simply the lack of light. Even as an atheist I believed that every living being has "goodness" in its true nature, and that "bad" people don't have evil at their root; they are just horribly disconnected from that inner essence of goodness.

I smiled when I realized that the new concept of God I was exploring was more like the Force in *Star Wars* than the human-parent concept of God I'd left behind ten years ago. Could it really be that simple?

I wrote on and on, examining my experience during those three days of hyper-awareness, and how it related to the concept of God. During those three days, I had been more in touch with my intuition than ever before. I was being prompted from the inside as I went about my day. I didn't make decisions or consciously try to figure out where to go, what to do. I was temporarily free of the voice in my head that usually guides my decisions and actions. I was just following what I felt an inner nudge to do. The nudge came as a wordless sensation in my chest or gut, whereas the voice I'd followed up until that point had always spoken from within my head.

I knew that that nudge of intuition had always been there; I'd just never felt it, or listened to it, as acutely as I had during those three days. Before that, more often than not I had actually overridden it with the loud voice in my head! I could remember times when I was partying at bars with guys or drinking with friends when I'd come up with crazy ideas of where to go or what to do next. There was often an inner inkling, a sense that maybe this idea wasn't so hot. But when I was drinking it was always "Game On!" It was so easy to ignore the little whisper, the nudge. I wondered if that was how animals went about life, without a constant stream of words in their heads, but just going with the nudge. Maybe it's the most natural way to live. Just feeling that inner guidance and acting from there.

It was plainly obvious to me too, knowing that my body is only 5% of my entire identity, that my circumstances, the actions of others, even the food I ate, weren't shaping my body and relationships. It was my thoughts and beliefs about how all these things affected me that were the true creators. It's like I'd been running on auto-pilot, living by default and not accessing the power of my focused thoughts to change my outer reality, and that was why I'd always thought I needed to change diets or jobs or boyfriends. My journal filled with example after example of how the thoughts and beliefs I'd held for the last 30 years had created my physical reality, not the other way around.

When I finally got tired of journaling, I called Grace. I wanted to know what she thought about all the ideas of God that were occurring to me. Her instruction had been to decide to follow the guidance of something bigger than my own self-will. Well, what if I gave following the nudge of my intuition a try? It had certainly worked during my three-day mental silence, but I'd never really prioritized listening for it before. I'd always chosen to calculate and figure out what to do, rather than just get quiet and intuit it.

Grace was open and excited about my new ideas. And I think she was a little relieved that she wouldn't have to battle me on the God issue after all.

She explained that, in her mind, the intuitive nudge that I was describing is actually God's whisper. She told me if I chose to listen to that little whisper, it would shift me from living from my head to living from my heart. It sounded a little cheesy to me when she put it that way, but still, something about living from my heart appealed to me.

"It doesn't seem like a big switch until you start really living it," she explained.

Well, if making that little switch would enable me to experience once again the heavenly inner peace I'd felt for those three days, I was up for it. Though I couldn't foretell the impact of making that decision to deliberately switch from living mind-based to living heart-based, it ended up turning my entire life around.

chapter four

mending the past

"Your vision will become clear only when you look into your heart. Who looks outside, dreams. Who looks inside, awakens."

— Carl Jung

*a*s time went on and I progressed in my recovery program, the experiences of mental quiet started happening more and more often. Before I'd done any of this inside-job emotional work—which was up until about my fourth month sober—I hadn't been sleeping well. Part of the problem in the beginning was trying to sleep without the help of alcohol, and part of it was my anxiety about all the work the recovery center people were going to make me do.

I usually slept from about midnight until 4:00 a.m., and those early morning hours were tough to get through. My mind spun and spun with worry and regret and fear of what was to come. The volunteer-of-the-year compulsion was coming out in me, and I asked the recovery center if I could come early to the morning meetings to help set up the room. They gladly accepted my offer to help, and I was glad to escape the torture of being alone with my thoughts.

One of the first times I showed up early to set up chairs and books, I met a guy named Hank. He was a grandfatherly type, a sharp-as-a-whip war vet who missed nothing. He and I were usually the only ones setting up the center at 6:00 in the morning, so we got to know each other a little bit. In fact, he was the only person I knew who was awake at 4:00 a.m. when I'd often be unable to sleep. He would always take my calls at that time of the morning and sometimes drive over and take me to the Santa Monica Pier to get me out of my lonely apartment. We would walk around the usually hectic tourist attraction in the pre-dawn quiet until the lights came up on the famous Ferris wheel at five o'clock in the morning, when he'd take me home to get ready for the day.

Those early morning walks saved me many times from falling back into depression. One of his favorite questions when seeing me was, "What's up, Dina? Your head botherin' ya again?"

The first time he asked me that question it stopped me for a moment. I was about to laugh and agree with him, but his question made me realize something. This head of mine, which was in fact bothering me, was just a bunch of thoughts; it wasn't my identity. I'd always believed the voice in my head because I'd regarded it as being me—but what if it wasn't? What if my thoughts were nothing more than words rolling around in my head that I could choose to listen to, or to tune out?

I took that analogy with me and tried to become, as Eckhart Tolle describes in *The Power of Now*, the watcher of my thoughts. The idea was to put some space between myself and the voice in my head to avoid becoming swept up by my mind. Surprisingly, it worked very, very well and gave me some relief. On some mornings, when the voice was particularly mean to me, I gave it an accent! I morphed the voice in my head into a cartoon-character voice or a British or German or Australian accent. It made it just a little bit easier not to take it as seriously. But I still kept showing up earlier than necessary to set up for the recovery meetings or to go for walks with Hank. It was still more effective to get out of my lonely apartment and distract myself from listening to the voice altogether.

Six months or so into working with Grace on the recovery program, the time came for me to confront my past. To write down the names and the story of anyone and anything I had ever held a grudge against or was fearful of, and to determine if there were people I'd hurt along the way so I could contact them to make it right.

Grace told me that my grudges and resentments were nothing more than "that which was blocking me from God." I rolled my eyes at first at the ridiculous simplicity of this idea. Any grudges I held were there because people had wronged me, you see. I wasn't going to let go of them because I was right, and the people I resented were wrong. Wasn't that the most important thing, to determine right from wrong and make sure justice prevails?

Grace smiled knowingly at my balking. I got the sense that she'd seen this from others she'd coached before. "Nothing can block you from accessing your God or your intuition, Dina," she told me. "What you're not seeing clearly yet is that you have a part in all of your resentments. It was your own disconnection from God—not following your intuitive guidance—which got you in a place where these people on your list could offend you to begin with.

"It's not so important who is right and who is wrong," she continued. "Staying in that mind-spin will keep you forever disconnected from God. We've identified your old idea as 'being right is most important.'

Are you willing to replace that with the idea that being connected to the voice of your intuition is most important?"

Tough call. But again, Grace's confidence won me over and I agreed, soothing myself that I didn't have to take her ideas on forever, but just for this time while we were working together.

So I began the exercise of taking at least an hour a day to look back over my life and write out all the resentments and grudges I could remember ever feeling. Once I started, the memories just poured out of me. I remembered feelings I had had about other kids in grade school and even jealous feelings about my sisters. I worked my way up through the years, and as I wrote these resentments and grievances down, page by page by page, it became crystal clear to me that they were my reasons for drinking.

I drank to soothe the pain of my perception of being wronged and the shame I had felt deep down when I had acted spitefully to get back at whomever I was nursing a grudge against at the time. Only in clearing out all these grievances with Grace's help did I see them for what they really were: my futile attempts to get from others what could only be found within myself: a sense of worthiness. That was what I had always been trying to get my hands on—but in all the wrong ways.

My mindset and attitude for many years had been self-righteous and closed-minded, though I didn't realize it. I was so empty inside that I had taken from others to try to fill myself up. Of course, that never worked, and all I ended up with was regret and guilt for some of the things I'd done along the way.

A few weeks later, after I had finished writing down every resentment I could think of, the rubber was about to hit the road. I had to set things right with the people I had wronged. To say I dreaded this is an almost comical understatement.

When I finally shared my list with Grace, I told her everything, even my darkest secret, a teeny tiny incident from years back that I'd previously thought I'd be taking to my grave. I'd stolen money from a prior job. At the time I had believed I was underpaid, and since my boss wouldn't pay me better I decided to take it for myself. My mindset at the time was that I was completely justified in stealing money here and there because, in my eyes, the organization was taking advantage of me and I shouldn't let them get away with it.

The people I worked for never suspected what I was doing, and for me to come clean was to put myself at risk of facing legal consequences, having everyone at my old job know what I'd done, and maybe even going to jail. No one had ever found out what I'd done and I wanted to keep it that way. I reasoned, why dredge up something from so, so long ago? Wasn't it better just to let sleeping dogs lie?

Predictably, Grace laughed at this justification.

"Dina, when are you gonna get it that drinking wasn't your problem, it was your solution?! Your problem is all these little secrets you're keeping. If you don't clear everything out and set it right, you are doomed to end up right back where you were, not all that long ago."

When I voiced my rationalizations out loud to Grace, even I could see how weak my justification had been in stealing and how skewed my thinking was. It was rather funny how "right" I thought I was. I'd been practicing following my intuition for several months at this point, and my gut was chiming in with Grace and also telling me I needed to make it right. And I saw very clearly what Grace meant about drinking being my solution. The anxiety about telling my old employer was terrifying, and a drink sure sounded appealing. In spite of my fear, I wondered what it would be like not to have the burden of the secret anymore, no matter what the consequences were.

Grace was sympathetic but very stern. She had gotten really good at the tough love approach with me. She suggested that I use my mini-meditations to prepare for the conversation with my former boss. My meditation practice was pretty strong by this time. I'd started referring to it as my "3x3" since I was consistently meditating for three minutes, three times a day. Just sitting and turning my attention inward, whether counting my heartbeats, noticing my breath, or observing and letting go of my thoughts. Grace told me to ask inwardly during meditation for the willingness to have this talk.

"Don't make the call to schedule this conversation until you are ready," she said. "Your time in meditation will prepare you. Even if it takes six months, don't jump the gun just to get it over with. It's important that you become completely willing to handle any consequences without resistance."

Six months sounded good to me. What a relief! No hurry getting thrown in jail on my part.

The day after my talk with Grace, I began preparing. In my mind's eye during my 3x3s, I visualized contacting my old boss, arranging a meeting and bringing a check to repay what was never mine to begin with. I visualized being criticized and publicly humiliated in front of people I used to work with. I pictured the cops roaring up to handcuff me and haul me to jail, sirens wailing so everyone would know I was a criminal.

In my mind's eye I saw myself calling my family to tell them why I was in jail, and asking my neighbor to feed my cat. I left nothing out in my mental prep for the biggest conversation of my life.

I'd been planning on six months of 3x3 visualizations to feel in my gut like I was ready and completely non-resistant to any consequences— to feel complete acceptance of what I'd done and to have let go of the shame and guilt. Grace had explained to me that my self-hatred for what I'd done just upset me more and was blocking me from accessing my intuition.

"Dina, you can't get an honest read on your gut until you let go of the anger you hold toward yourself."

I knew she was right and I poured myself into my visualizations, seeing myself being punished and facing consequences in my mind's eye, while accepting that they were my due. At first it was very painful, and I thought it was going to take months and months of visualizing to break through to any sense of peace. But I was very surprised. I felt I was completely ready to make my amends after only four days.

This was the first time I experienced the power of my little minimeditations in handling a real life problem.

I called the organization and made an appointment to meet with Becky, the woman I used to report to. Usually, before confessing to something that I'd done, I would have felt anxious, nervous, even nauseous. And I definitely would not have slept well the night before. But with my 3x3 prep, amazingly enough, I didn't have any of those symptoms. I slept well the night before our meeting and was able to eat a normal breakfast, even knowing I might be going to jail in a few hours. I'd stocked my place with cat food in case my neighbors needed to take care of KC for awhile.

I was at a point inside myself where I'd let go of any resistance to the consequences. Picturing myself being taken away in handcuffs didn't upset me. The consequences weren't mine to choose. Once I fully accepted that I was in the wrong, I was ready to accept whatever response the organization I'd stolen from might have. I just knew, deep in my gut, that I was ready to have this conversation.

That morning, I arrived at my old place of work and was invited into Becky's office. She's a middle-aged woman, sharp and efficient, with a nurturing side I'd seen glimpses of in the past. As I sat down across from her, I felt a flicker of gratitude that I'd prepared as well as I had for this little chat. I knew I would already have been in a puddle of tears on the floor if shame had been dominating me in that moment. But I was ready. I couldn't change what I'd done and I was there to make it right.

When we were both seated, I got right to the point. I detailed to her exactly what I had done. Straightforward honesty and confession spilled from my heart. I was calm and clear on what I needed to say. When I was done, I felt that whatever Becky deemed to be the appropriate consequence was going to be OK with me. I'd said my part. It was all up to her now. My palms weren't even sweaty as I reached into my purse and presented a check for the amount I had stolen and awaited her decision.

Becky looked me squarely in the eye and didn't mince words. "I would have had to fire you if you were telling me this while still an employee," she said. "But since so much time has passed, it's all water under the bridge. I don't want your check. There was another person who did the same thing awhile back, and he got caught. We fired him on the spot but didn't ask him to repay the money. So that's how I'll handle it with you."

Her response left me speechless and I could barely control the tears pricking at my eyes. Becky stood up and I did too.

"Dina, you are not a bad person," she said, more gently than I felt I deserved. "Doing this does not make you bad. You're not a bad person trying to get good. You're a sick person getting well. And I'm very, very glad that you're on the path to wellness."

I was in awe of Becky's depth of understanding and kindness. But even stronger was the sense of peace and freedom that I felt in that moment. And the most amazing thing to me was that I had felt this peace even before our conversation. It almost hadn't mattered how she would choose to handle it; what was important was my readiness to accept her decision no matter what it was. In a way, I didn't even need her words of comfort; I had felt completely at peace with everything even before our talk.

As I drove home, my mind was utterly silent. Silent like those three days in February. There were no words in my head for several hours after our talk. Usually while driving, I'd be jabbing at the radio buttons, frustrated that I couldn't find a good song, or I'd be so distracted by my mind churning a mile a minute that I'd arrive at my destination with no recollection of how I had gotten there. But on this day, my drive was different. I was back in a hyper-present state of mind, absorbed in the beauty of everything.

Along the freeway, trees gently blowing in the wind captivated my attention with their surprising beauty. They seemed to sparkle, as if they were lit up at Disneyland. I could barely keep my eyes on the road I was so enamored with the trees. I felt so connected, so at peace within myself and so in love with all of life and all living things. Tears poured down my cheeks as the feeling of freedom sung within me.

I arrived home that afternoon and immediately made an anonymous donation to a charity in the amount of the check Becky had refused to take. I felt relieved as I donated it. That money was not mine to keep.

That wasn't the only tough conversation I needed to have. Next hardest on my list were the former boyfriends I needed to make amends to. So that's what I tackled next.

In preparing for each of these conversations, I used the same technique as the first time and visualized all the possible outcomes every day in my 3x3 meditations. One of the most important things Grace had pointed out as she helped me prepare for these chats was that I knew what *I* had done, but I had no way of knowing what impact I'd had on the other person. So when the time came for me to have each conversation, I made it a point to ask the person if there was anything that I'd done to hurt them that I might not be aware of.

When I asked that of some of the guys I'd dated, more than one of them tactfully told me that I had been emotionally draining to be around, and that they felt like the attention or affection they gave me was never enough for me. They were frustrated because they didn't know what more they could possibly have done to make me happy.

It stung to hear those comments, but in each raw and honest conversation, I listened and came to a complete acceptance of their words. And with each one, I became freer and freer on a deep level inside myself. This was only possible because I had prepared so thoroughly for each conversation. If I'd still been holding a grudge while apologizing to an ex-boyfriend, I would have missed out on my own healing.

It was crucial that I was in a place of neutrality and openness, completely having let go of any resentment, hurt or anger, before I could go back and amend my own actions and attitude. Otherwise, I would have just been setting myself up for a heated argument rather than a healing conversation.

Before you've met your soul mate, people say, "You'll know when you know," and I like that phrase for this kind of thing too. I just knew when I was ready because I wasn't bracing myself to deflect hurtful words or undesirable ramifications; I wasn't afraid of them in the first place. The conversations went through me rather than bounced off me because I didn't resist what the people told me. In a few cases I cried. Sometimes a lot. But when the tears subsided, so did the pain. I let myself feel all of it, every emotion, for the first time in my life…and then I was done.

Through the process of mending my past, it became obvious that most of my depression and unhappiness had come from my own fear of feeling an emotion fully. I was afraid to let it wash completely through me without numbing or controlling it. What I found through this experience was that even negative emotions can't last forever if you let go of all resistance to them.

When I could face the possibility of the worst losses and outcomes with no resistance, I discovered that I was free. Fear and resistance had been my enemy for all these years. Released from their grip, I could begin to re-create my life.

chapter five

the damn laundry

"He who cannot change the very fabric of his thought
will never be able to change reality."

— Anwar al-Sadat

t was at a barbecue with sober friends one afternoon in the summer of 2009 that I first met Jesse. She was in her early 50s, but her long brown hair and contagious smile made her seem much younger. Her carefree laugh could be heard a block away. Intrigued by her sense of lightheartedness, I went up to her and introduced myself. After talking with her for just a few minutes I could say that, without a doubt, she was the happiest person I'd ever met.

Chatting with Jesse, I felt inspired but also a little suspicious. Someone this happy might not have her feet on the ground, or might even have a few screws loose. At the same time, though, I couldn't help but notice that I felt more alive after just a few minutes of conversation with her. At the end of our chat I asked Jesse if she'd mind taking a walk and getting a coffee sometime since we happened to live in the same neighborhood. She readily agreed, and the following Saturday found me walking to her place for our walk-and-talk.

When I arrived at Jesse's door, she greeted me with a big "Hello, Dina!" accompanied by an exuberant laugh and a warm hug. She grabbed her handbag and we took off on our walk. I'd never witnessed a person with this energy level, this zest for life. It kind of overwhelmed me, but at the same time, I sensed there was something I could learn from Jesse.

We walked down near the beach, along bustling Main Street in Santa Monica. Jesse's attention was easily grabbed by passing dogs she stopped to pet, storefront displays with lovely, expensive clothes, and restaurants with sumptuous menus posted along the sidewalk. Everything in her eyes was "Wonderful!" or "Magical!" or "So exciting!" I felt like I was walking with a giddy five-year-old trapped in a grown woman's body. It occurred to me that we needed a place to sit down and chat to reduce the distraction factor.

The coffeehouse we stepped into was busy, but we found a small table and settled into it. When our orders arrived, I sipped my iced tea and got down to business.

"Jesse," I said, "you've got to tell me. What is it that makes you so happy? No one I know has this kind of innocent energy, this crazy love for life. What is your secret?"

"Well," Jesse said with a gleam in her eye, "it's very simple. I just don't do anything until I feel like doing it."

This was not what I was expecting, and I was disappointed. I could see that it was totally consistent with her childlike energy, but it seemed a highly unrealistic way for busy folks like me to live.

"Wow. I guess you don't go to work every day," I said with a mischievous smile.

Her laugh seemed to come from the core of her being.

"Oh no, I don't work, but that's not what I mean. I just take the time to get into alignment with whatever it is that I'm going to do, and I don't take action until it feels right."

This intrigued me. I needed examples.

Her face lit up. "Here's one! A good example is my running. I love going running every morning, but it wasn't always that way. Years back, it was a struggle to exercise, to motivate myself to run or to go to the gym. Through my meditation practice, I got myself in alignment with wanting to go running, and then the running took care of itself!" She gave a happy shrug.

Well, I've definitely prepared for scary conversations with people in my meditations, but getting excited about running five miles six days a week? Not so much.

I asked Jesse for her advice on things I dreaded doing in my own life. "There are some days I just do not want to go to work. Or to the grocery store. Or do the dishes or the laundry."

Laundry was a big one. I've always particularly hated washing clothes.

"Jesse, I want to know how to be happy while I'm doing all these things that I have to do but don't want to! What would you do if you were me?" She was starting to feel like my guru-next-door.

I got the big laugh I was coming to expect after any question I asked her. It seemed to delight her that I thought she had some secret that I wanted in on.

"It's not a secret! Just don't do anything until you feel like doing it! That's my only rule. You should try it! You really should." She smiled and winked.

Yep, just as impractical as I expected. I wanted to protest: *Don't you know I work full time?! Am I supposed to call in sick when I don't feel "inspired" to sit at my desk?! And, by the way, it used to take at least a half-bottle of wine for me to even begin thinking about doing laundry!* I didn't see how I'd ever get anything done if I chose to live my life her way.

Meanwhile, Jesse was reading my mind and interpreting the sideways glance I was giving her. Another hearty laugh.

"Oh, Dina, I'm not telling you not to do anything until you feel like you're walking on clouds. I'm telling you that your first priority before taking action of any sort is to meditate and visualize yourself doing it successfully, which will bring you into alignment with the action and, with time and practice, will provide the inspiration that will let you get your mundane chores done with a lot less struggle."

I didn't believe her. I thought she must live in some la-la land where clothes wash themselves and leprechauns push through the mounds of paper at the office.

But something inside me stirred and interrupted my cynical thoughts. I did want to have access to her joy in living, after all. This was the only rule she had; if I could live by only one rule, I'd like that. I decided maybe I'd try it. And I'd try it first on the damn laundry.

"So," I asked, "how would you advise me to get my piles of laundry done? I've skipped it the last couple weeks because it just feels like a giant burden. I keep putting it off, and now it's overwhelming me. I ran out of socks four days ago!"

Jesse laughed and I continued. "Part of me knows it's so hard only because I'm thinking so negatively about it. I want to change the way I'm looking at chores that I don't like but really need to do every single week. I've *always* hated doing the laundry and waited until I'm absolutely out of clothes and have no choice. But it would be great to be able to keep up with it so it doesn't become such a huge task."

"Well," Jesse said, "just take time in your meditations to visualize going through the motions of this dreaded task and enjoying it. Then after a few days check to see if you still feel overwhelmed about it and go from there. Even if you're still not excited about the laundry, I bet you won't mind it so much."

I decided to take on Jesse's idea as a challenge. I wasn't planning to skip out on work or anything; I resolved to visualize one thing that I dreaded doing until I got to the place where I felt like doing it. And, damn it, I was going to start with the stupid laundry.

I sat for my usual three-minute meditation that afternoon after my walk with Jesse. I closed my eyes and breathed for a few moments, then pictured myself spilling my piles of laundry all over my bed and sorting everything into manageable piles. Then I pictured myself stuffing the first batch of clothes back into the laundry basket.

As I looked through my mind's eye, the sun was out and the laundry machines in my apartment building were available and working properly. That alone was half the battle. I saw myself starting the water in the washer and pouring the soap into the basin. I visualized the cool water washing over my hands feeling refreshing and then began to add the clothes.

Since I only had three minutes in my meditation, the cycle finished at lightning speed and I transferred the clothes to the dryer, feeling the dampness of the fabrics and the vibration of the machine as I put quarters in and started it. The dryer finished instantly in my mind's eye and I pulled the clothes out, folding as I went. My favorite sweats felt warm and soft; everything was clean. I hung and folded all my clothes, and I was done.

My timer rang and my three minutes were up. It wasn't half-bad imagining doing the laundry, though it felt kind of ridiculous to deliberately visualize it. I got up and went about all my usual weekend errands, but I wasn't quite ready for the laundry. One more week without clean clothes wouldn't kill me.

Well, the week flew by and Saturday rolled around. That meant it was finally time to get my towering heap of laundry done. I'd been doing my laundry visualizations three times a day all week and over the past couple of days, I'd actually found myself looking forward to sorting through my clothes. I sat for one more three-minute meditation before I pulled the overflowing laundry basket out of my closet, and I was finally ready to get started.

When I got to the laundry room, I started the washer and watched the water steadily fill the basin. I uncapped the bottle of detergent and breathed in its pleasant fragrance. I filled the cap and poured the detergent slowly into the running water, watching bubbles form in the pool below. I pulled my clothes out of the laundry basket one at a time, sock by sock, shirt by shirt, and added them to the machine. As each garment went in, I watched the swirling water engulf and saturate it.

I closed the lid and left the basket on top. I wanted to sit outside for a while.

My cement stoop was cool to rest against and a refreshing contrast to the warm sun. I sat back and listened to my music playing through my open front door. Out of the corner of my eye I saw two tiny white butterflies chase each other around a tree. What fun little beings they were to watch! Their wings fluttered effortlessly as they played their chasing game. KC walked outside onto the stoop to stretch out and lay next to me in the sun.

It occurred to me how much had changed in my life and in myself over just the last few months. Not that long ago I wouldn't have been able to even start the laundry without half a bottle of wine swimming in my veins. And here I was, actually enjoying taking my time, getting it done and even just sitting outside. My intention to stay present while doing this chore had the positive side effect of keeping me aware enough to enjoy the tiny butterflies. I liked where this was going.

Half an hour later, I heard the washer clunk after its final cycle. I transferred the clothes to the dryer, just as I'd visualized so many times. I added the quarters and hit the Start button, and the machine began humming and vibrating immediately. I leaned against it for a moment, feeling the motion transfer into my body. I felt like meditating again, so I went back inside and meditated for three more minutes. Sometimes I would do this and end up meditating four or five times in a day. I always did the three regular ones at about the same time each day, and an extra like this one wouldn't count as one of my normal 3x3s.

After an hour, the dryer clicked off. I walked back out to the laundry room, feeling the sunshine on my face. I was completely at ease with what I was doing. During my meditation, I'd been picturing my warm, scented clothes fresh out of the dryer. Now, in real life, I opened the dryer and took each item out slowly, one at a time, folding and stacking each one carefully as I went. There was no rush to this, nowhere else to be. This was my big laundry day and I was enjoying it.

I went back into my apartment and shut the door behind me. One of my favorite songs was playing on the radio. I looked around and felt deep appreciation. *Look at all that I have*, I thought. *My home, my clean warm clothes, my favorite music.* Back in my bedroom, I emptied the contents of the laundry basket onto my bed. Transferring the clothes to hangers was so sensual! I couldn't believe I'd never noticed the different textures of the clothes that lay against my body every single day.

Appreciation flooded through my being and I started dancing. Alone at home. Dancing and hanging up my clothes. Twirling through the room to the closet and hanging them up, one at a time. I could have stacked them up first, more efficiently, and then carried them to the closet, but it was fun to dance while I was doing this. I hung the last skirt and closed the closet door quietly. The song had changed; the music had turned mellow. I leaned against the closet door and felt the tears coming.

Waves of sheer joy poured through me and I swooned about my apartment, letting the tears come and wanting to move about at the same time. I just felt so happy, so in love with my life. On paper, to the outside world, my life might not look all that different than it was the last time I did laundry. My neighbors wouldn't have noticed me washing my clothes any differently than usual. But on the inside, nothing was the same. Transformation and true happiness had taken root within me.

I thanked Jesse silently for helping me turn my most dreaded chore into magic.

chapter six

k a t e

"What 'love' is I don't know if it's not the response of our deepest natures to one another."
— William Carlos Williams

One morning at the recovery center, I was approached by a young, forlorn-looking woman as the group was dispersing after the meeting. A tall, thin blonde, she told me her name was Kate. She was very pretty but I could tell she didn't think so. Her hands were shaking badly; she was still going through drug and alcohol withdrawal. She told me she'd liked some of the things I'd shared about myself and my recovery in the meetings and asked me if I would be open to having a coffee with her sometime.

My heart went out to Kate immediately. I remembered all too well my first days in recovery, shaking as if I had a perpetual chill I couldn't warm up from, overwhelmed and apprehensive. I told her I'd be more than happy to meet up with her and help her in any way I could.

At our first meeting for coffee, Kate asked me if I would play a mentorship role to her as she tried to get stable in sobriety. I was surprised when she asked me that; I'd only been going through the recovery center's program for about eight months at that time. I knew the center encouraged people who had gotten stable in their own lives to coach the newbies just coming in, but I didn't think I was anywhere near being able to do that yet. I wasn't sure how to answer her, so I told her that I'd talk to my coach that night and see what she thought. If anything, maybe Grace could take Kate under her wing.

That night I called Grace and asked her what she thought I should do. She immediately asked me, "Well, what do you think you still need to accomplish before you'd be ready to help someone else?"

Hmm, now that was a good question. "Well, my biggest problem is that I want to lose these ten pounds I've gained, bingeing on sugar since I quit drinking. I need to decide what diet to start on and what gym to join so I can jump-start this health kick."

And in Grace's classic tough-love, not-taking-any-backtalk way, she said, "Dina, you are more than ready to get out of yourself and help another addict."

And that was that.

Kate and I began meeting up with each other regularly. Sometimes we met at a coffee shop; sometimes she came to my apartment. She liked seeing and playing with KC, which I took as a good sign. I liked people who liked my cat. She had lots of anxiety about getting sober, having tried to stop drinking and using cocaine lots of times over the past couple of years but never getting it to stick for longer than a few weeks. In talking with her I realized how unbelievably far I had come in the last several months. I started to feel like maybe I really could help her out with the process of facing her past and weeding out the demons that had been driving her behavior.

At one of our first meetings, Kate wanted to talk about God. She asked me what my concept of a higher power, or God, was.

"I used to think of God as a parent or teacher," I said. "Someone who rewarded me for obeying Him and doing what He wanted me to do, and punished me when I didn't. But all of that has changed. I don't think of God as an outside entity now; I just think of God as the best part, the innermost essence, of all living things. It's an energy that's inherent within us and we can either live our lives expressing this loving energy to others, or we can cut ourselves off from it—but then we're miserable.

"It's pretty simple in my mind, actually," I continued. "You can see this intelligent energy in yourself if you just look for it. If you get a cut on your skin, your body knows how to heal it. If I got pregnant someday, I wouldn't have to figure out how the baby is going to develop eyes and fingers; it's taken care of effortlessly. It's the same power that keeps my heart beating while I sleep at night. It's what grows a complex flower from a simple seed. It is an energy of life and wellbeing and healing that everything in the universe has access to, and is born from."

This was simple and obvious to me, but it was a bit nebulous for Kate. She said she preferred the idea of God as a being that she could talk to and interact with, rather than a vague energy source. She was comfortable with the God she'd learned about in her Christian home and loved since childhood.

"Kate, that is great!" I exclaimed. "The concept of what or who God is doesn't matter in the least. What matters is your intention to align yourself with God or cut yourself off from God. You can choose any form of God you like!" I told her that Grace had even told me that my higher power could be a doorknob or a tree. "As long as it's not you, your brain or your willpower," I said, echoing Grace's words.

My explanation satisfied her. I asked her if she was willing to prioritize listening for the quiet voice, the inner nudge, the voice of God, rather than continue as she had been these last few years, following any and every loud compulsion, but rarely the small, steady whisper.

Kate was very willing to try this. She said, "I've always believed that's the right thing to do, to follow my conscience, but it's never the fun, exciting thing to do, so I got used to ignoring that voice and following these wild impulses that always got me into trouble." She paused for a few moments, mulling something over. "Why wouldn't I just follow God's voice in the first place if it's the best thing for me? How come I've become so good at ignoring it and making crazy, impulsive, aggressive choices instead?"

Well, now, wasn't that an excellent question. Jeez, where was Grace when I needed her? I didn't have these answers. I didn't have nearly the wisdom that Grace had had with me when I was asking her all my questions.

"Um," I stuttered, "well, I know when I was drinking so much and going out and doing stupid things, I was feeling so hollow and empty inside that I was looking for anything to ease that feeling and make myself feel even just a little bit better. Somewhere inside I knew I wasn't doing the best thing or the right thing, but I didn't care. I was selling out just to get the instant relief."

"Yes!" Kate agreed. "That's exactly right." She spoke reflectively, articulating her realization as it came to her. "I've done all these things just trying to escape myself. I didn't know where I was going; I just knew I didn't want to be where I was."

Wow, did that ever ring true. Flashbacks of job switches, apartment changes, boyfriend upgrades, and better cars inundated my mind. I had never cared where I ended up either, as long as I could escape where I was. "Isn't that funny, Kate. Me too."

Then Kate asked, "Dina, how do you know when you're connected with your higher power? I am feeling so cut off from God, and I'm just not sure how to get that connection back."

I remembered that feeling vividly. It had been nearly impossible for me to see the light at the end of the tunnel when I was so deep within it.

"You might think that you need to work to get yourself back in connection, but it's kind of the opposite of that," I said gently. "You need to relax into it and accept that some unpleasant things are going to come up, or even expect them and let them come. What's torturing you is your resistance to all the feelings that are coming up. Once you surrender and just let the bad feelings wash through you, you will get some relief and be able to get through it."

I took a deep breath, thinking of the misery I had been in. "It's like the release you feel inside after you have a good, hard cry. You might resist crying at first, but finally you just get to the point where it takes you over. And once it's done, you feel a little bit better."

I had another thought. "See, we resist crying because we don't want to feel any worse, when actually, if we just give in to it and let ourselves feel it completely, we don't stay as stuck and we can move on and feel a little relief.

"Why do you think you drank and snorted so much coke? I know when I was drinking so much, it was to numb those painful feelings. So it makes sense that all you want to do is avoid feeling them. But the way you get back into connection with God is by going through those feelings, not avoiding them like you've been doing for so long."

Kate thought for a few moments and then said, "I felt pretty close to God in the beginning when I first stopped using drugs, but after the last week or two of writing out my resentments, I've felt like God is deserting me, or even punishing me by making me relive all of this.

I've been hoping that, once I'm done, He'll come back to reward me for pushing through this."

Kate's conception of God was different from mine, but she was describing the same experience I'd had. While I was writing all of that stuff down, access to my inner source of peace had been overshadowed by all the loud voices of resentment and anger that I was poking around at. But once I had given the voices their chance to speak, acting as their scribe, and then shared it all with Grace, they had dramatically subsided. Since then, my access to my intuition was largely unobstructed.

"Kate, these resentments are what's blocking your access to God. Once they're released, you'll feel close to Him again. God isn't any further from you than normal, there's just more clutter in the way of getting to Him right now." I was trying to choose words she'd resonate with. An analogy popped into my head. "Picture it like there's a channel or a gateway through which God communicates to you. If that channel gets clogged up with resentments, your access won't be restored until it's cleared out. That's what the writing is doing."

Then another angle occurred to me. "God doesn't disappear and then reappear. God is steady. It's our access to God that fluctuates. Just because you can't feel God doesn't mean God isn't there. And the people on your resentment list are there because you looked to them to fulfill something for you, when really all you needed was connection to your inner God source. No human in your life is ever going to be able to make up for that lack of connection."

Kate's expression clouded with confusion. I realized she was still muddled in the hell of finding and releasing resentments and couldn't see why this process was helpful just yet. My heart filled with compassion for her. Not that long ago I wouldn't have understood this either. I'd felt like I was underwater and couldn't figure out which way was up.

"Kate, don't worry about understanding all of it now. Just know that God is always there. And trust this process. I promise, you will have better access to God than you've ever had once you've cleared out the emotional clutter. Just take it one resentment at a time, one meditation at a time. That is how you'll get this done."

Kate's expression relaxed and she said, "That makes sense." Then she wailed, "I just wish it was over with!"

I laughed. I completely understood. I had felt the exact same way.

Kate left our meeting with a lightness about her. I smiled inwardly and was inspired to sit down to write a little list of things I was grateful for.

For several months, Kate and I met up every week or so. She adopted my little 3x3 meditation practice and asked me to hold her accountable to it. I agreed to and found that it helped me too. When she would text me three times a day as she finished her meditations, it kept me on track for my own 3x3s. She was in the habit of calling me almost every day, and I was beginning to feel close to her, like she was my little sister. Technically, I was helping her, but in doing so, I was getting so much out of it. It was very satisfying to have someone ask how I came to have the peace and happiness I had, and then for me to be able to explain how it had happened and uplift her and encourage her from my own experience.

In all my years of volunteering in hopes of finding fulfillment by giving to another, nothing had ever given me even a fraction of the fulfillment I was getting from mentoring Kate. Maybe this was my "calling," to work one-on-one with people who have been where I'd been, to contribute to others not just with donated clothes and food but with the benefit of my experience, my personal awakening. The crazy thing was that I felt like this whole process of mentoring Kate was bigger than both of us. Talking with her brought out the best in me; it literally felt like my innermost essence, my Big Me, was communicating through me and drawing out the best in Kate. I'd never had a relationship like that, and I'd never experienced anything as fulfilling.

Kate and I were in a comfortable routine of meeting every week and talking on the phone when she wanted to in-between. This was the same arrangement I'd had with Grace. In all my months of working with her, Grace had never once called me. She had told me in the very beginning that this was the way it had to be.

"I love my life now," Grace had said, "and I walk the path I choose. And if you want to be on that path with me, Dina, it's up to you to put forth the effort necessary to keep up with me. In order for me to stay steady and on track myself, I can extend my arms to you from my path, but I cannot leave it to come find you and bring you to it. The desire and the effort have to be generated by you."

At first that had seemed harsh, but now I'm extremely grateful that she handled me like that. If I had been able to draw her into my self-pity and misery, it wouldn't have served either of us. Only when I was really ready to change, which for me meant hitting bottom not once but twice, was I willing to leave behind the drink and change my behaviors and my thinking. Grace was the right fit for me because she had been there too and completely understood all of my struggles, but she wouldn't let herself get dragged into the drama of it. Fortunately, at that point I finally wanted what she had more than anything, so I had been able to put all of my energy into following her instructions and keeping up with her.

So far I had made my best effort to take the same tactic with Kate. I'd let her initiate all of our meetings and phone calls and did my best to bring her focus back to where she was going and away from the comfort of self-pity. Weeks turned into months and her progress was ticking along.

Then, one afternoon my phone buzzed with a new text message. I figured it was Kate checking in on completing a meditation, but that wasn't what her text said at all. She wasn't completing a meditation or asking a question about God. Nothing of the sort.

She had texted me to let me know she was drunk.

Oh. My. God. I couldn't believe it. My breath left me for a moment. I re-read it to make sure that it was indeed from her and that it did indeed say that she was currently drunk.

Where did I go wrong?! How could this happen?! She's been doing so well!! How did I not see this coming?! The voice in my head wasted no time piping up that I was an utter failure as a mentor.

I had a compelling urge to text her back: "Where are you, I'll come get you, stop everything, get back to the recovery center! I'll help you, I'll make it right!" An angry swarm of self-loathing thoughts consumed me. *What the hell are you going to do?! You idiot! You blew it!* The inner voices attacking me and urging me to go find her and save her were loud and insistent. *Maybe I should go get her; what if something happens to her that I could prevent?! Shouldn't I go dry her out and get her back on track?!*

These thoughts paralyzed me for two full minutes. Then my mind suddenly cleared. I remembered, *Oh yeah, this is not how I handle things anymore.*

I'd had enough experience by then to know that my mind's loud, compulsive voices weren't generally the voices of inner wisdom.

Grace! I needed to talk to Grace. Right away. I picked up my phone and dialed her. Voicemail. I dialed again. Voicemail. I texted her. Nothing. I waited a few minutes for her to respond. Minutes felt like hours while I stared at my silent phone.

Okay, I told myself. *You know what to do. Grace always says feel your way through it, don't think your way through it.* Well, I'd already dismissed all my first compulsive thoughts. So at least I knew what *not* to do. But I had no idea what on earth I should do instead.

I needed to get quiet. I went to my couch and sat on the very edge of it, as I always did when I meditated. I set my phone's timer for three minutes, breathed deeply, and began my meditation. In my mind's eye, I texted Kate back, begging her to tell me where she was so I could come get her and help her. I pictured her not responding to my texts and calls. I visualized myself driving around town to different bars looking for her. I saw myself hauling her out of a bar and taking her home against her drunken will. None of these felt good in my gut.

I breathed again. I knew I could find the answer. I knew it was there in the silence, which was hard to find in that moment. My focus narrowed slightly. I started to regain control of my scattered mind. I breathed deeply, releasing my tension and willing myself to be open to the solution and to doing whatever I needed to. *Please just guide me*, I asked inwardly.

I re-set my three-minute timer a couple of times. I was determined to find direction from my intuition before I responded to Kate. After the third round of three-minutes, my eyes shot open. I knew exactly what to do. I remembered Grace telling me before I ever met Kate that I can't make another person drink any more than I can keep them sober. However much I may want to keep them from drinking, it is not in my power. I realized that I was a source of strength and guidance for Kate, but she needed to seek it; otherwise she wouldn't be able to receive it.

I picked up my phone. It had been about fifteen minutes since she texted me. I typed a reply, "It takes what it takes, Kate. You are loved beyond measure. Do what you need to do. I'm here when you're ready. I cannot leave my path for you, but there will always be room for you here on my path."

I read it over twice, judging by my gut if it felt like the right response. After a moment, I pressed the Send key.

I spoke Grace's wisdom in my mind: *I walk the path that I walk and when Kate chooses to walk next to me, then we walk together. When she does not, then we part ways.* Could it really be that simple?

Actually, yes, it was that simple. Refreshingly simple. I have to stay on my own path and I can extend my arms to another, but if they are beyond my arm's length, they are too far off my path for me to be of any help. If I leave my path, I disconnect from my own source of wellbeing, and without my wellbeing, I have nothing to give. Maybe that's why the flight attendants always remind us to put on our own oxygen masks first before helping others with theirs.

I thought it through. If I had blindly followed my loud mind's instructions and insisted on finding her and drying her out and she resisted, I would have ended up resenting her for being ungrateful, and she would have resented me for trying to control her. If she hadn't resisted, she still would have missed the self-empowerment of finding her sobriety for herself.

A basic truth became crystal clear to me in that moment: Sobriety is mine because I want it. I am sober for no other reason than that I want to be. I can't force anyone into wanting anything for themselves.

Surprisingly enough, within minutes I was at peace. I had let Kate go completely. I didn't resent her and I was letting go of being mad at myself. I felt nothing but compassion for her, and I held a mental image of her in her wellness, not in her sickness.

This was a brand new experience for me, to let a person go without any strings, even a person I had spent a lot of time with and really cared about. In those few minutes, I had unintentionally peeled away another layer that deepened my freedom. It wasn't how I would have chosen my path with Kate to go, but I felt like I was going to be OK.

Days went by and I didn't hear from Kate. I wondered about her but didn't send her another text to follow up, much as, in some moments, I wanted to. I knew that it had to be her decision as to whether or not she wanted to keep going in the same direction I was headed. I had no idea if I would ever hear from her again, and that was hard. But I would be here for her whenever she was ready.

It was her choice.

chapter seven

oatmeal cookies
for breakfast

"Metabolism is vibrational response to your moment in time. Metabolism is the way the energy is moving through your body, you see. And so everything is in response to the way that you feel. Everything is mind over matter. Every disease is mental first. Everything is about thought. Everything is about vibration."

— Abraham-Hicks

Shortly after I became comfortable working with Kate, my attention turned toward losing the extra weight I'd been putting on. By fall of 2009, I hadn't had a drink in months, but I sure had made up for it with food. Grace had told me in the very beginning not to worry about my diet for a while. She told me to conquer the drink first; the food issue could be dealt with later. Many times I'd kept myself from picking up wine at the grocery store because of the permission she'd given me to binge out on chips and cookies instead. I had even been justifying having cookies for breakfast if they had the word "oatmeal" on the package.

But after several months of unrestricted junk food, my weight was catching up with me. I was wearing stretchy skirts and yoga pants most of the time since I had gained a size or two and couldn't fit into my usual pants or jeans anymore. In fact, one guy at work had asked me in a hushed whisper if I was job hunting, going out on interviews during my breaks, because I was dressing in skirts all the time.

Something needed to be done.

I've always had a love-hate relationship with food, with the emphasis on love. Before I discovered alcohol's magic, food had long been my go-to cure-all when I had time to fill, wounds to nurse, anxiety to quell or boredom to beat. In terms of diet, I've tried just about everything over the years. Any time my weight shot up by three pounds, I called in the reserve troops. Something had to be done, pronto. I tried the high-protein diets and the low-fat diets. After my cholesterol went up, I swung to a vegan discipline, cutting out all meat, dairy and other animal products for a while. Have you ever tried vegan cookies? YUM! Lots of pastas, breads and unbuttered bagels are vegan too! I actually gained weight being vegan because I steered clear of the vegetables that most vegans center their meal planning around.

Trying to make up for my excesses, I've done lots of cleanses too. I've guzzled cayenne pepper lemonade for days on end and limited myself to raw veggies for seven-day stints here and there, just to name a couple favorites. I never followed any of these dieting regimens as they were designed, though. When I got excited about a new diet idea, I bought ten books on the subject, read a few paragraphs in each and figured I could take it from there. Not surprisingly, none of the diets or cleanses that I did "my way" were ever effective. Usually I ended up with ravenous junk food cravings and gained the little weight I'd lost right back.

Around this time a friend mentioned that she was getting acupuncture to help with her sugar cravings, so I decided to check out a student clinic nearby. My Needle Lady, as I referred to her, assessed my symptoms very thoroughly at our first meeting and was very gentle as she stuck the needles into my skin, here and there, all over my body. She even applied these small bumpy stickers on my ears, explaining that I could squeeze them whenever I felt a sugar craving. After a few sessions, I thought it might have been working a little, but I wasn't entirely sure. Even with all the needle sticking and ear pinching I was still experiencing some strong cravings.

Then, finally, it occurred to me that if visualizing during my 3x3s had helped me get over my laundry issues and fear of tough conversations, maybe it would work for eating healthier too. I began using my mini-meditations to picture eating and enjoying healthy stuff like vegetables, salads and green tea. It was a rough start for the first few days—very hard to picture enjoying all this wonderfully healthy food. Nothing was changing in my mindset. Junk food still seemed way more appealing than a boring salad. I wanted to believe I could come to love veggies, but I also couldn't fool myself, even in my mind's eye. Time passed and I couldn't bring myself to genuinely enjoy the visualization.

So, I came up with a new tactic. Since I'd become very confident in relying on my intuition, I figured maybe I could intuit what to eat, rather than plan it logically. I reasoned that my body probably had an instinct for what would be best for me to be eating, so I started spending my 3x3s visualizing myself tuning in to that voice before I went food shopping, or as I looked over a menu in a restaurant.

It only took about three days for me to start getting in the groove of it. To my surprise, it was actually fun! The visualization was definitely most enjoyable when I put my attention on discovering what my body was really hungry for, beneath the cravings. It made sense to me that there must be a steady voice of healthy food preferences in there that my demanding sugar cravings had been drowning out. I didn't visualize eating anything in particular; I spent my 3x3 time just tuning in to being able to hear my intuitive urges for food.

I also began extending my visualization to seeing myself eating the food that my body requested, and feeling it assimilate into the cells of my body, strengthening each organ and muscle, and morphing my body into its strong and lean natural state. Visualizing this way felt great. I even noticed that my thoughts about my body were changing. When I saw a woman with a lean, healthy body like the one I wanted to have, I didn't have the usual jealous, critical thoughts. Even before I lost a pound, I found myself thinking, *You look great! We could be twins—my body looks as good as yours!*

I came to really enjoy this; I was getting pretty good at listening to my body tell me what it wanted to eat and also how it wanted to exercise. I knew that my body was born with a blueprint of optimum health, and for the first time ever, I was listening to it tell me how to follow that blueprint and take care of it in the best possible way.

The next development was that I began to see how important my feelings were in my meditations. I had learned that visualizing loving salads didn't make me crave them. I could tell it wasn't working because the meditations didn't make me *feel* any better. I started to notice that the way I felt in my visualizations was more important than what I was visualizing. I needed to find a visualization that felt better, and I started experimenting to see what worked.

Right away I discovered that I really enjoyed visualizing feeling strong and beautiful in my body. I pictured myself wearing my favorite jeans again, after months of not being able to get them over my hips. Then, I started picturing my favorite jeans being too big for me! *Look how great my body looks*, I thought during my meditation. *These jeans that I've worn for years are actually too big on me!*

These visualizations felt so good I focused on them entirely for a few weeks. I didn't change anything else. I didn't eat a particularly healthy diet or start a big workout or do any detoxing. I ate what my body indicated it wanted, but already the sugar cravings weren't running me. Cheesy as it sounds (no pun intended!), at the grocery store I asked my body inwardly, "What do you want to eat?" The answer was there if I just stopped to listen to it. I felt healthier right away doing this, as if I had lost the weight before I even lost a pound.

This was similar to the experience I had had when I visualized my interaction with the former boss I had stolen from. I didn't give myself a deadline; I didn't use my mind, brainpower or willpower. I simply *felt* my way through it, rather than thinking my way through it.

To my amazement, it worked. It took probably about three weeks until something clicked inside of me and I began feeling as though I was skinnier and healthier, even before anything happened to my body physically. That was the key: feeling like I'd already achieved my goal before I made any physical progress. Once that switch flipped and I achieved that feeling of peace and success, it only took ten days for seven pounds to fall off my body. I know that sounds unbelievable but my body literally responded that quickly once I began feeling like I'd already lost the weight.

It was completely effortless; I had used zero self-discipline regarding food. The only discipline I kept was in my 3x3 visualizations: doing them at least three times daily, and focusing intently on how I felt with my new, healthy body. Plus, I found that it continued to work over time. Unlike with the diets I'd attempted in the past, the pounds stayed off exactly as long as I kept feeling good in my body. As

I meditated, I felt as if I were programming my ideal body weight into my brain, and once I started to feel that I'd achieved it, I began to see the results physically.

I did find that if I wanted to maintain the results I had achieved I needed to stay consistent with my visualizations. I quickly learned that, as soon as I lost my strong-healthy-lean mindset, the weight would come back. But it was easy to get back on track by focusing on the feeling of a lean, healthy body during my next 3x3 meditations. I found over time that my body responds very quickly to thoughts I hold about it, whether they are negative or positive.

I have another visualization that I do right before eating at a restaurant. No one ever knows I'm doing it but, as everyone looks over the menu, I take a moment to tune within and be inspired to choose the food that my body's cells want for nourishment right then. I think of my body as an intricate organism that requires premium fuel, and I want to provide that. And after I choose and order my food and it arrives in front of me, I take a few seconds to visualize this food being processed perfectly and becoming one with each cell of my body as I ingest it. My cells know exactly what to do; my only job is to listen to them and follow their instruction on what fuel to take in. So simple! And much easier than the weighing and measuring and all-around torturing of myself with dieting.

And sugar cravings? They used to run me. I was their slave, and their loud voices completely drowned out my intuitive voice, so I never even knew it was there. Now I focus on accessing that inner voice before the craving can get the upper hand. By doing so, I plant a seed in my mind that changes my mindset toward eating. I've learned that cravings aren't physical; they're mental. Even though they translate as a very physical compulsion to eat vast amounts of junk food, if I'm in a good place mentally, junk food loses its appeal and kind of falls off my radar.

As I began to have success with this visualizing-to-lose-weight idea, I was reminded of a couple of other times in my life when I had shifted my mindset and literally changed my body. Until this point, I had never given a second thought to these incidents, but now they made perfect sense.

The first incident happened in the winter of 1996 in Galway, Ireland. Let me preface this by saying that, throughout my childhood, I came down with strep throat two or three times every winter without exception. All through high school and my first two years of college, that trend continued predictably—until the semester I studied abroad. I was in Galway when the first round of that winter's strep throat hit me hard.

I'd never gotten sick in a foreign country before and finding a doctor and figuring out the insurance and finally getting the antibiotics that I needed (when all I wanted to do was curl up in bed) put me over an internal limit. I decided then and there that I would never, ever get strep throat again. I knew I was due for at least one more round of it that winter, but I told myself I wasn't going to allow it.

I made that decision in one moment, and do you know what? I never did come down with strep throat again. I've been around people who had it, I've even felt it coming on, but it has never taken hold in my body. If I feel it coming on, all I do is take my attention completely off the fact that I might get sick and tell myself, *I'm healthy and my body knows how to stay that way. I used to be a person who suffers from strep throat, but not anymore.*

Sounds too simple to be effective, I know, but it really did work. In that moment of pain back in Ireland when I made the decision, I knew in my bones that I'd never come down with strep again. I know now that what becomes physical starts out as mental first, and as long as I remove my attention completely from sickness and keep focused exclusively on health, my body will stay healthy.

The second experience happened just a few years ago. I had a painful experience at the dentist, and I decided that my teeth and gums would become one of the healthiest areas of my body. I didn't start brushing my teeth obsessively 12 times a day or do anything different at all; I just made the decision that I never wanted to experience that again, and I just knew that I wouldn't. It's been about six years now, and I haven't had a cavity since. In fact, my gums used to bleed during my regular cleanings and check-ups, and even that hasn't happened in almost six years.

It occurred to me that there might be some other explanation, an X factor that I hadn't picked up on, or maybe it was all just coincidence. But another part of me knew that there was something to this, that making decisions about what I would allow to happen within my own body was working, even though I didn't know why. It wasn't until I began my 3x3 visualizations, though, that I started to see just how powerful the mind really was.

chapter eight

k c

"It is not the meaning of life we are seeking, it is the experience of being alive."

— Joseph Campbell

K C stands for KittyCat. This is the clever name of the little creature that had been living with me for more than nine years by the time I got sober. When I first met KC, a nondescript gray tabby cat, he was emaciated and had lost over half the fur on his scrawny body from fleabite infections. He was so gross I was hesitant at first to be a part of the rescue squad with my neighbor Mike, but my sympathy for the poor cat finally won me over. Together we were able to catch him and take him to the vet to get cleaned up. Then Mike and I took turns feeding him, and KC gradually learned we were not a threat and made his home in our adjacent yards.

I'd never been a cat person and KC did not impress me at first. For the first few months after he became healthy, he spent the day outside, then came in for dinner when I got home from work and slept inside on my bed. When I moved out of that place, I was going to leave KC with my neighbor, but as I was packing Mike said, "KC has grown fond of you. He's really your cat now; why don't you keep him?" So I did. And that's when I began forming a relationship with him.

I tried to imitate his meows so that we could communicate, and I gave him treats whenever he vocalized. This turned him into quite the chatty little guy. My boyfriend at the time, when witnessing us "talking," would playfully roll his eyes and whisper to KC, "Don't encourage her."

KC got pretty smart about chatting for treats. When he started to get fat, I stopped giving in every time he chatted. There were a few times when he meowed so much he lost his voice! Then he got clever and efficient. The moment I'd walk in the door from work, he'd use his "hoarse meow," pretending he'd been screaming for hours waiting for food. I slowly started falling in love with his little mannerisms and personality.

As time went by, KC and I got more and more on the same wavelength. He responded when I called him over to snuggle with me or save me from a spider or told him "no" or "stay." I asked myself sometimes if it was possible to have a co-dependent relationship with a cat. There were several times over the years when I turned my intense thoughts away from suicide because if I were gone, who would take care of KC? I loved that cat more than I loved some people. I wish that were an exaggeration, but it isn't. At a time when I was pretty wrapped up in my own troubles, he gave me something outside myself to focus on.

KC had been with me since before I drank heavily, during the full-blown alcoholic times, and for these first few months in sobriety. He'd met all the boys, heard all the dreams, soothed all the tears, shared all the joys. He had witnessed the diets, the resolutions, the job changes, the persistent quest to find out if this is really all there is. And he kept me steady through all of it. He was my rock; if I had nothing and no one else, I still had KC.

Until I didn't.

In late September 2009, I arrived home from work one day and noticed that KC's leg was swollen. He'd been outside the day before so I wondered if maybe a bee had stung him. I took him to the vet to get it checked out and she was alarmed immediately.

Dr. Sue was a warm, motherly type, with long salt-and-pepper hair that gently framed her face. She ruled out the possibility of a bee sting and took some X-rays. She wasn't getting any answers so she decided to take a biopsy sample and run some tests, promising to call me as soon as she had the results.

As promised, a few days later she phoned and asked me to come back to the office with KC to talk about his test results. That sounded ominous. Fear gripped me and I couldn't stop my hands from shaking as I packed KC into his carrier and drove over to her office. Dr. Sue led me into the back office as soon as I arrived. Compassionately but matter-of-factly, she told me that my baby had a wild, extremely aggressive cancer that had started in this swollen leg but was progressing rapidly. My body gave out and I sank distractedly into a nearby chair. I didn't know what to say and at the same time I had a million questions.

"What should we do? What can save him? What would you do if KC were your cat? What is best for him?"

With great gentleness and compassion, Dr. Sue began to explain the options in detail. I felt shocked and overwhelmed. I just couldn't believe this was happening. I barely heard anything she was saying and she soon realized that.

"Dina, why don't you go home and let this all sink in? We don't have to make any decisions tonight. Call me tomorrow and we can go over all the options then." I thanked her and left the office.

On the drive home I felt like my world was rocking off-balance. For the first time in quite a while, I wanted a drink. I wanted a gigantic glass of my old friend, my red wine. My mind was out of my control and reeling with catastrophic predictions. Just one glass. Please? Just one.

At home I let KC out of the carrier and he immediately ran into the kitchen, chattering away like usual, begging for food. My heart melted and tears pricked at my eyes. For some reason, the sight of him begging for food like nothing was wrong prompted the thought, *I don't need wine. I need my three minutes of meditation.* And with that thought, I realized something important for the first time: I had always turned to alcohol because it quiets my crazy mind. My whole, entire life-long problem was the unrelentingly pessimistic, fearful and critical voice in my head. And wine sure was an effective remedy for that.

But now, so was my meditation. At least it gave me some space around my thoughts. So I fed KC, sat quietly and breathed deeply for three minutes, and then got up and went about my evening at a safer distance from a drink than I had been four minutes earlier.

The following day I called and talked with Dr. Sue about how to handle KC's diagnosis. I agonized with her over the decision of how to treat his cancer. I'd always thought it was crazy the lengths people would go to in order to keep a pet alive, and now here I was in that exact mindset. Money didn't matter, the only thing that mattered was what would give KC the highest quality of life for the longest amount of time, with the least amount of suffering.

Throughout our discussion, though, my gut didn't feel at peace with the radical treatment options. My mind asked the vet a dozen questions, but my heart didn't really need the answers.

After many tears and much thought, Dr. Sue and I decided not to do anything extreme that would deteriorate KC's quality of life, even if it would extend it. Somewhere inside me I felt a small release, a sense of relief. I didn't make the decision with my head; I made it with my heart, and I knew it was the right path to take.

My tears were still streaming as I hung up the phone. I felt like I'd aged 20 years in those last 20 minutes. KC was curled in a ball, a sleeping furry angel on my couch. I knelt on the floor and put my arms around him, burying my face in his fur. He turned his head, yawned and licked my eyebrows, like he always did. I held him and told him I loved him and I would do anything he needed me to. "Just tell me what you need, KC. I am here for you. I'm here for you now, just like you always have been for me."

I flashed back to the moment months earlier, when, sitting with KC on this very couch, I had had the experience of knowing that all would be well when his time came. I sure didn't feel that way at this point, but I still trusted that that experience was true. Everything would be okay. Everything was already okay. I just couldn't feel it in that heartbreaking moment.

———

As the weeks progressed, KC and I were on a frequent vet-visit schedule so they could monitor his progress. Over mere weeks, the cancer spread to his lymph nodes and his heart, and his leg became badly infected. I took him to the vet every other day to have the bandage changed. He whittled himself down to seven pounds. He couldn't eat cat food anymore so I fed him Stage One Gerber baby food. But he was still eating. And he was still using his bad leg when he'd jump onto the couch or the bed to cuddle with me. It wasn't time to say goodbye quite yet.

Throughout this time I'd been relying heavily on my 3x3 meditation to keep myself sane and calm. I visualized every possible decision, each and every outcome. I visualized caring for him long-term, buying special food and medicine, and, finally, having him leave my world. With each session I felt myself let go of more resistance, and release into a willingness to accept what I was seeing. It didn't take that many meditations to come to complete willingness. The key wasn't the time I was spending, it was the strong desire I had to be in the place of non-resistance and acceptance. And I got to that place. As I became more open to what was to come, I became more able to know when it was his time to go.

I knew it wasn't my choice to make; it was only my job to recognize the readiness in him. My meditations were what some call prayer. I kept the channel of access to my intuition open and put forth my readiness and intention to be of service to KC with whatever he needed. My focus was on feeling his energy radiating toward me as I'd felt it back in those three days last February. I knew he was communicating with me, and I was tuned in to that, feeling my way through it.

On the first of December, 2009, I knew it was the day. The night before, he'd slept next to me on my pillow, and I had known the time was very close. But on the morning of December 1st, something felt subtly different in my gut, and I just knew.

I called the vet; we planned for one o'clock that afternoon at my apartment. I arrived before she did and opened my front door to sit in the sun on my front stoop. KC had always loved his sunbeams; he hobbled out to catch some rays with me for a little while.

Dr. Sue arrived. She was the perfect person to facilitate this moment. She was compassionate and nurturing and gave me all the time and privacy I needed to say my goodbyes to my baby. I knelt next to him and wrapped him in my arms. I cried and cried and I held him tightly to me. I locked eyes with him and told him I loved him for the last time. When my tears subsided for the moment, I reluctantly moved to the side and let the vet squeeze in next to us. She stroked his fur gently, but he didn't respond to her touch. "It's his time, Dina. KC is ready," she said softly, her voice full of sympathy.

She gave him one injection that put him to sleep. I was streaming tears but very present, very intent in the moment. As KC went to sleep for the last time, he looked again into my eyes and gave my nose two last little licks. I knew that I was doing the right thing. The vet gave the second injection. He left his little body so peacefully. Nothing happened that was any different from him just falling asleep.

As Dr. Sue wrapped him in the blanket to take him, his paw covered his little face; he had loved to sleep like that. It was done. He was gone.

The vet hugged me tightly, tears tugging at the corners of her eyes too, and then left with KC.

I looked around my apartment, alone for the first time there. I took his drooled-on rainbow catnip toy and his food dishes and put them outside. He'd loved that stupid rainbow. I couldn't bear to have his things inside anymore. I saved a bit of fur the vet cut for me in a tiny jewelry box. I didn't want to be at home, not in that empty apartment alone.

I walked down to the beach. My tears continued to stream but I was not weeping. I walked slowly and I took in the details. I saw every tree, every flower. I was intensely present. My mind was still. An emotion washed through me of deep love, deep connection. I could feel the life energy of the trees I walked past. Lately I'd been noticing that in moments like this, when I was fully present, I sensed the trees communicating with me, or maybe I was picking up on their communications with each other. Not in words but in energy. I felt unity, oneness, and comfort as I slowly continued on the path to the beach, touching the bark of each tree along the way.

My emotion became more intense and I began to feel absolutely complete, at one with life, at peace with death, in complete acceptance of the circle of life, content in letting go. I was deeply serene. And after the feeling of acceptance washed through me, I felt bliss. I don't know if I'd ever felt bliss before, but that's the best word I could find to describe it. It wasn't a far-reaching, out-of-this-world feeling; it was actually just a step beyond what I had felt moments before. Yet it was another layer, a new spiritual muscle being flexed for the first time.

I wandered to Starbucks and got my favorite coffee. It was the holiday season so they had their special cups with little feel-good messages printed on them. Mine said, "… see the world not as it is, but as it could be…" Something clicked. I really got it. To see the world as it "is" would be to squarely face the cold, hard fact that KC was dead, that I would never see him again, and to wallow in self-pity and dwell in the loss. What I was experiencing was what the world "could be"—interconnected, universal, with death being nothing big, just the next step after this physical life was done. For each on his or her own timetable.

I walked on further to sit on the beach and look at the water. I felt the sand, really felt the sand between my toes. Tears came and I let sorrow and grief take me over. The depth of my sadness washed completely through me. I was unafraid of my emotion; I welcomed it. I welcomed the relief that raw expression of emotion provided. I wept and wept. And when I was done, when my tears ran dry, at least for that moment, I walked home.

Home was different; it was heart-breakingly quiet. No hoarse meow, no greeting of any kind. KC's food bowls weren't where they were supposed to be. Everything was different. This was the exact moment I'd been dreading for the last nine years. I had been through loss before, but not like this. I felt a wave of gratitude that this hadn't happened a year earlier, when I was planning my suicide. I definitely would have drunk heavily and maybe would have gone through with taking my own life, with my excuse for sticking around no longer here.

I wondered if maybe KC had sensed how much I needed him and hung around to get me through that time. When I had first started falling in love with KC all those years back, I had warned myself to be careful not to get too attached, all in an effort to protect myself from this exact moment. But as I actually experienced that moment, I knew there was something to the old saying, "It is better to have loved and lost than never to have loved at all."

I was grieving, but nothing was wrong, really. All was well and would always be well in the completed circle of life.

chapter nine

video games

"The invariable mark of wisdom is to see the miraculous in the common."

— Ralph Waldo Emerson

In the first few days after KC died, I was more subdued than normal. I even found myself preferring silence while I was driving, instead of the usual mindless search for something I liked on the car radio. My morning ritual was now to do my 3x3 last thing before I left my place and got in the car. The lingering inner silence from the meditation made driving a much calmer experience than I was used to. My mind was quieter, so I was able to hang onto the inner feeling of openness that I always experienced during and after my 3x3.

With the radio off and my mind calm and open, driving was tolerable and even pleasant. Usually all I ever noticed on my commute to work were other cars and pedestrians, but beginning in this handful of days I started noticing other things. One morning I saw for the very first time a row of bright pink and yellow buildings that I must have driven by a million times. How had they escaped my awareness all this time? I must have been pretty wrapped up in my own head not to notice such a striking landmark.

Then I started noticing the trees. Along one stretch of a main road near where I lived in Santa Monica, there was a row of one-story pink buildings with a row of young five- or six-foot trees lining the sidewalk. The morning sun cast vivid shadows of the skinny, leafless trees onto the pale pink buildings, and the image popped out at me and took my breath away. I felt like I'd never seen anything so beautiful, so perfect, in my life.

My attitude toward driving completely changed. I began looking forward to the silent drive every morning so I could see my skinny tree shadows. Even more than the way they looked, it was the way I felt when I was looking at them that I liked so much. They were so perfectly formed and arranged they gave me a feeling of being in touch with a divine sense of order or harmony. I wondered why this strip of street wasn't used as a movie set, it struck me as so breathtaking.

I savored these experiences—connecting with nature, noticing the birds perched on telephone wires, admiring a wise, old tree while walking to the beach. It was like I could really see for the first time. Like a Hollywood re-release, my world seemed to go from black and white to rich, textured, brilliant colors.

One afternoon I found myself back in old thought patterns of frustration with traffic and other drivers, and I realized I was back in a dark cloud where I couldn't see the beauty in my surroundings anymore. What used to be normal driving frustration was now so distinctly different from how I'd gotten used to feeling while driving that I made it a priority to try to get it back.

I had the idea of looking at driving as if I were playing a video game. As a driver in a game, you would expect obstacles and be on the lookout for them; you wouldn't rage at them. Navigating around them is what gets you points! You actually want them to pop up so you can score and also get better at the game. And you'd never take any moves by others personally, or wonder what on earth they were thinking. Instead, you value them, seeing them as challenges that keep you sharp and adept at playing the game.

Practicing video-game driving helped me see how big a difference there can be between what is actually happening and my perception of what is happening. Instead of obstacles being bad, they're a training tool. Instead of other drivers' motivations being infuriating, they're kind of irrelevant. It was a real eye-opener for me to see that I have that wiggle room; I don't always have to let my "default" perspective dictate the same old, predictable responses. There is room to change, room for relief from the usual stresses.

While imagining I was a driver in a video game, I had another experience one day when a particular tree with its leaves dancing in the wind caught my eye. I was already in a good mood, and this tree looked so strong and healthy, it seemed like I could feel the wellbeing it was exuding. The leaves were literally dancing in the strong wind, and as I got closer to the tree, I could tangibly feel joy radiating from it. As I crossed right in front of its path, looking straight at it, I just knew that it was laughing! It was not a victim of the wind; it was having a blast, joyously dancing with the wind! In fact, it was drawing the wind toward it purposefully so that it could dance and move around.

I knew that the tree was aware of me too. Half of its leaves and branches ducked behind a street sign as my car approached and shot back up high in the air as I passed by, blowing wildly in the wind. *That tree was playing peek-a-boo with me,* I thought. It was plain as day that the tree was clearly bursting with pure joy and letting me know it was aware of me and including me playfully in its world.

I know, I know. Sounds nuts. But when I'm in that state of mental silence and connection to life, I am able to peer into the perspective that these trees live from. That playful tree reminded me of my three days of mental silence back in February, when KC and I had exchanged so much affection just in our gaze alone. Words were entirely unnecessary since everything could be communicated with our eyes and the energy of our being acknowledging each other. Now I was realizing and directly experiencing that trees and flowers have as much character and intention as dogs and cats and people.

Since then, I've been able to feel the energy of trees and flowers every time I intend to. I love tuning into the energy of animals and plants because they have very little resistance and, for the most part, radiate purely joyous energy. It's all a matter of personal experience, just as there are people who don't recognize that dogs, cats, cows and pigs have distinct personalities, and others who can easily see it. Of course, it's easier to see animals' personalities since they're able to show affection and trees don't in the same way. But sometimes the very slightest breeze will move a flower or some leaves almost imperceptibly, and if I'm looking for it, I'll be able to feel the energy it's radiating.

What I believe is happening is that, when I'm in a state of alignment with *my* innermost essence, I can see the innermost essence in all living beings. I'm using the word "see" and for me it is a visual experience—it looks like tree trunks and flower petals have a very fine, sparkling glitter on them that is infinitely perfect and beautiful.

I know it's not technically accurate but I call it "seeing in 4D" when I'm in that state of awareness. It's as though a veil has been lifted from my eyes so the essence of every living thing that I see comes into sharp focus and connection. Time doesn't exist—I have no perception of (or need for) past or future—when I'm in that higher consciousness state. The usual feeling that I am separate from the things around me fades, and the truth of my oneness and connection with all is plainly obvious and immensely satisfying.

I find I can see the essence of other beings most clearly when I maintain a state of meditation while at the same time doing routine activities like driving and walking. While my conscious mind is distracted with the task of driving, I feel inwardly silent. In this silence is where I feel the essence of trees, animals, and people. When I see and feel it within myself, I can see and feel it around me too.

These experiences enable me to be able to see our human bodies as nothing more than vehicles carrying around our life essence. My physical self is just like a 3D avatar in a computer game, a form or body that I animate with my mind's intention. Of course, it's a higher version of that because it's a form that carries around our being, our light essence—not just some electronic impulses. Still, it helps me keep perspective when I'm seeing my body as a very cool vehicle with which to navigate life.

Another visual experience that began to happen during these heightened awareness states was that I started seeing other people's bodies as avatars (or finger puppets animated by Big Me as I described in Chapter 3). Everyone looked kind of like a robot to me, in both their face and body. Not in a lifeless, zombie-like way, but in a "that-is-SO-not-their-identity" way. When I'm in this state, I see human bodies as amazing vehicles, so beautiful to see moving about. And when I see people in this robot way, almost everyone looks asleep! I could be having a perfectly lively, coherent conversation with a person and just know that they are fast asleep. It's not that their eyes are physically closed, because they aren't, but to my innermost self, they are. In the same way that trees don't really have glitter on them and yet that is what I see, these people are wide awake and yet I see their eyes as drooping closed. I think it's just my perception of others not being in the same state of awareness at the same time that I am. If they were, I'd imagine I would see them as awake.

While I am in this state, every person, animal, tree and flower is intensely beautiful and easily lovable. A pure love radiates from deep within me and I can feeling it reaching deep within them. In fact, when I watch TV or movies I often wish the camera angle would pan out so I could "see" the loving, positive Big Me energy behind the face and body better. A close-up on just their face gives me such a small view into the person's self. Even if someone's behavior or words are far from positive and loving, when I keep my attention focused on their Big Me, that's what I see in them.

There is only one thing I need to remember in order to be able to see everyone's underlying essence. The key is to keep an awareness in the back of my mind throughout the day that every person I interact with has light and love at their innermost core, no matter how obvious it may or may not be in the moment. I look only for that innermost essence and allow everything else to fade in importance. No matter how annoying or frustrating a person seems to be, they still have that light and love in their core. And the more I look for their beauty, the more I see it.

Maybe not surprisingly, it was easiest for me to see the essence in people I barely knew or had just met, rather than in those who had been getting under my skin for years. Once I got the hang of it with people I felt neutral about, I wondered if it would work with people I had a closer relationship with, or with people who had been annoying me for some time. If I could focus only on the core of light and love in the people who are challenging for me, I'd find the ultimate freedom: I would no longer be controlled by what anyone else was doing, but instead solely by who I was being.

I believed that when I let the light and love of my essence express itself fully, that is exactly what I would draw from others. The exciting next step would be to test out this new theory.

chapter ten

pre-forgiveness

"We awaken in others the same attitude of mind we hold toward them."

— Elbert Hubbard

My 3x3 had proven effective in so many ways, from preparing for hard conversations and getting dreaded chores done, to eating better and losing weight. I wanted to see what else I could use it for. Besides having chores that I dreaded doing, I also had people in my life whom I dreaded interacting with. And yet I knew that these people possessed the same innermost light as the people I enjoyed being with. I wondered if I could use my 3x3 to find that light in the people who rubbed me the wrong way.

I started with a guy I know, a friend of a friend, whom I had just flat-out never liked. He wasn't a bad person; he'd never done anything horrific, I just felt extremely defensive and uncomfortable whenever I was around him. I had met him on several occasions, usually when out to dinner with our mutual group of friends.

Here's the thing about this guy (I'll call him Gary): whenever we ended up chatting, he always found a way to undermine what I said or made me look stupid in front of everyone else. One time he looked me up and down and said, "Dina, you have such a cute little body. Why do you insist on wearing clothes a size smaller than you are?" His greatest talent is his remarkable ability to come up with zingers that drill straight into my insecurities. I'd always tried just to ignore his comments or laugh them off, but I boiled inside every time. Sometimes I wished I had the courage to tell him exactly what I thought of him.

So when I got invited to a dinner party that I knew Gary would be attending, I had the perfect opportunity to try using my 3x3 to prepare for our interaction. The day before the party, I was out at a coffee shop with my super-happy friend Jesse and had the thought to also pick her brain on how she would handle this. How did she stay happy dealing with people who got under her skin or were just plain mean?

As predicted, Jesse laughed out loud at my dilemma.

"Oh Dina, you can't control people! You can't control your environment, and you really have very little control over how people act toward you, what they say to you. But," she said, looking me in the eye, "you also don't have to play their game. If he tosses a ball to you and you don't throw it back by getting all upset, there is no game."

"I know," I said, "but I still wish that he would change and stop saying awful things like that. Who says that to people, anyway? I have no idea how he has any friends in the first place! I hate feeling anxious around him. I wish I could buy an emotional bullet-proof jacket someplace."

Another gigantic Jesse laugh. "You've got to get to the place inside where you are so content with who you are, so happy with yourself, that comments like that just roll off your back. The problem isn't what he's saying to you; it's how you let it get under your skin. Let him worry about who he is, and you just worry about who you are."

Jesse leaned back and smiled at me. She seemed to think she had taken care of the problem nicely. But I felt frustrated by her lack of specifics on exactly how to do what she was recommending. I wished she had an action step, or maybe the perfect comeback line I could use, instead of this happy-la-la-land-wishful-thinking advice.

Jesse just kept smiling and we sat in silence for a few moments while I mulled it all over in my head. I remembered how ridiculous I had thought her laundry suggestion was in the beginning, so I tried to stay open-minded that this tip might actually prove to work, even though I couldn't fathom how to do it. Maybe by using my 3x3 I would gain some sort of clarity.

Back at home after our walk, I sat down on the edge of my couch. This had become my most comfortable meditation position, just by trial and error. I'd come to like sitting with my feet flat on the floor and my back straight, not resting against anything. I began my visualization with the intention to use it to prepare for the Gary Insult Onslaught. I directed the words in my head toward making peace with him.

Gary, I forgive you. I forgive you for all the times you have hurt me before. I know that if you were a truly happy, decent person it wouldn't give you this sick pleasure to torture me like you do.

Hmm, somehow that didn't sound like what I should be going for with this. The voice in my head piped up. *Damn it, Dina! All you're doing is being smug and getting a jab in at him, telling yourself you're morally superior and pitying him because he isn't blessed to be as kind to others as you are. Start over.*

I tried again and my timer went off after three minutes, but I really wanted to get this so I reset it for five more minutes and closed my eyes again. It's amazing how necessary meditation becomes once you do it enough. More time meditating and visualizing becomes as exciting as sitting down to popcorn and a movie. You're in for a ride and your only job is to watch and evaluate the image forming on the screen.

I conjured an image of Gary in my head. My mind's ears heard him insulting me, and my mind's eyes saw me not reacting, choosing not to jab him back. I pictured us in conversation and found myself wanting to be free of the desire to react to him. As I looked at him with my mind's eye, I said inwardly, *Gary, I am giving you all the space in the world to be or do or say whatever you want to be or do or say while you are in my presence.*

I giggled a little after I internally said these words. It was pretty cool being in charge of how people acted when they were in my presence! Funny as it sounded, it did kind of give me the illusion of control over my interaction with him when I gave him permission to be himself. I felt the knot in my gut loosen and release. *That's what you're going for, Dina,* I told myself. *You need to feel freedom, not anxiety, even when he is doing the very thing you hate most. That's good enough for now.*

I opened my eyes after the extra five minutes and felt markedly better than I had before I sat down. I still had four more 3x3s to work on this before the dinner the following night. *Maybe Jesse was right about this after all,* I thought. Whatever happened, it would be interesting to see how I would react toward him.

The following evening after my last 3x3 visualization, I left for the group dinner. I had gotten to the point where I felt neutral about seeing Gary; I could take it or leave it. This was a huge improvement over the way I had dreaded seeing him in the past. I'll take neutral over strong aversion any day.

I pulled up to the restaurant, parked my car, and once more thought the words that had been continuing to come up in my meditations: *Gary, I am giving you all the space in the world to be or do or say anything you want while we are at this dinner together.*

At this point I was really getting into my little game. I was looking forward to seeing how Gary would choose to act towards me with this "permission" that I'd granted him. Walking toward the front door, I got distracted by a beautiful old tree. Its thick trunk was textured and weathered, and I stopped to feel the bark and trace its grooves with my fingers. I looked up at the leaves and saw that they were moving almost imperceptibly in the calm air. Their motion stirred something within me. The tree was acknowledging me! The tree was exuding energy and I was able to pick up on it. It felt steady and comforting, wise and unburdened. My heart surged with emotion for this living being.

Tears started to burn behind my eyes, taking me by surprise. I closed my eyes and leaned against the tree for a moment, absorbing its energy and giving it my own. I felt complete, I felt connected, seeing the true nature of this tree. Nothing was more important in that moment than my connection with the tree. The words, *we are the same* floated through my mind. I stepped away from the tree and looked around at people across the parking lot, a stray cat hiding under a car. *We are all the same. I am them and they are me.*

Still in the midst of this awesome feeling, I walked into the room where my friends were already seated. As I walked by Gary, he looked up at me and said, "What's up, Little Red Riding Hood?" nodding with a smirk toward the crimson hoodie sweater I was wearing. My high was undisturbed. I looked him straight in the eye, which I hardly ever did, and felt myself completely let go of all my resistance toward him. Inwardly, the words of my meditation became real; I granted him all the space he needed to do or be or say whatever he wanted.

I consciously felt space too, between his comment and how I chose to let it affect me. With this breathing room, it was obvious that his little joke wasn't aimed at me; he was just trying to fit in by being witty. I felt like laughing! Not at Gary, but at myself for taking everything that people say so seriously! It's never been about me, no matter what anyone has said, or however specifically it has seemed to be about me. Gary's comment was just a way to try to make people laugh and to fit in with the group, and he would have taken that opportunity with anyone.

"Good seeing you, Dina, it's been awhile. Looks like stress has been getting to you, huh?" he rambled on as I stood there smiling at him. "Gray hair sneaks up on the best of us. If you need a good colorist I'm sure Lindsay can recommend one." He winked at our mutual friend with Kool-Aid-red hair.

I could barely contain my inner laughter! It's not that I found his comments amusing, and, surprisingly, my laughter wasn't coming from a place of pity that this guy was such a mess that he had to insult his friends to feel better about himself. My inner giggling came from realizing that none of this meant anything—and I've always made what other people have said about me mean *everything*. I was so strongly tethered to my Big Me in that moment that nothing around me was a problem, in fact, everything was colored by the warm glow of Big Me.

I had never felt so free! Words floated through my mind, making me smile. *I have complete freedom if nothing on the outside can budge my inner connection.*

I had a wonderful time that evening and laughed a lot, even at Gary's little jokes. And from that day, I began using this little "pre-forgiveness" technique on anyone who annoys me. Sometimes it takes nothing more than three minutes in my car before going in to meet up with the person. I spend those three minutes visualizing the first three minutes of our interaction. If I get overwhelmed I just remind myself that I only have to do this for a short period of time, for an hour or an evening or the duration of a meeting. Knowing that it is a temporary thing, a little game to play, makes it easier to swallow on some occasions.

As I play this game, I find that I am not just enduring or tolerating other people's words or actions, I am truly undisturbed by them. Their comments go right through me. I don't need to wish for a bullet-proof vest anymore because there is no danger from a verbal assault. The threat I'd been afraid of, criticism or disapproval, existed only in my own mind. When I realized that anything that anyone said was an expression of what was in them, not what was in me, I was free.

I had wished for more courage in the past, but this was so much better. There's no need for courage when the fear is gone.

I called Jesse to share all of this with her. She was absolutely delighted and since this had worked so well I wondered what else I could learn from her. My time working with Grace had come full circle and I was ready to learn from yet another new person with a new perspective. I asked Jesse if she would take on the role of coaching me and she readily agreed. I hung up the line a little nervous about what working with Jesse would be like, but nonetheless I trusted my intuition that it was the right next step for me.

chapter eleven

kate's back

"Pain pushes until vision pulls."
— Michael Bernard Beckwith

Wondering whatever happened to Kate? A few weeks after her drunken text, she arrived back on the sober scene. The first time I saw her back at the recovery center, we hugged and reconnected; it was so good to see her! She explained that she'd had a fight with her ex-boyfriend that had triggered her relapse. She was feeling stressed and anxious from her ongoing process of writing out all her resentments. I wished time would hurry up—or she would hurry up and get through her recovery program assignments. Everything would open up for her if she could just make it through this tough part.

Several days after she had re-initiated contact with me and assured me she was all dried out from the booze binge, my phone rang and it was her.

"Hi, Dina!" she said. "I need to vent. I cannot stop myself from thinking about Bobby, my ex. I almost called him about fifty times today, but I finally decided to just call you instead."

"How are your meditations?" I asked. It was always my first question, as it had been with Grace for me.

"Getting better," she said. "It was slow going there for a few days, but I'm finally getting back in the swing of it. But why the hell can't I stop thinking about Bobby? Is there anything I can do to get him off my mind? I really don't want to drink over this, but I don't know how else to deal with it." Kate had explained to me early on that she'd rarely been without a boyfriend since high school. Guys made her feel validated, cared for and loved. Many of them were also on her resentment list. "My thoughts are so crazy!" she said.

"Your thoughts are crazy, but they aren't you!" I told her. "That's how to deal with them: just watch how crazy they are without being attached to them or even really listening to them," I had told her this before but maybe now it would make sense. I described my tricks for separating myself from the voice in my head so I could be less under its spell. "Give that voice in your head a cartoon accent, and maybe you won't take it so seriously!"

We both laughed. "You know, that might help," Kate said.

"Kate, listen," I said. "Our minds are like magnifying glasses. Whatever you focus on becomes huge. For better or for worse, whatever you have your attention on keeps getting bigger the more you think about it."

"I know, I know," Kate lamented. "I need to work on letting it go."

I laughed out loud at that one. "Oh, Kate, I think my favorite thing that you say is 'work on letting it go.' Because working on something is the opposite of letting it go!"

On impulse, I abruptly changed the subject. Maybe she just needed to think about something else. "Tell me three things that happened today that you're grateful for."

"Grateful?" she echoed, taken by surprise. "Not sure if there's anything right now, actually." The line went silent for a moment while she switched gears mentally. "Well, I guess I'm grateful that I have a warm home and food to eat," she said vaguely.

This wasn't having the effect I wanted. I dug around mentally for an idea. "Actually, Kate, tell me three things that made you smile inside today!"

"Smile inside?" she echoed predictably.

"Yes! What happened that made you feel really good, that made you smile inside? Did you get a surprise call from your mom just saying she was thinking about you, or did something fun happen at work, or maybe drivers were nice, letting you in their lanes on the freeway?" I suggested.

"Well, hmm..." I could tell her gears were switching and she was getting engaged in the game. Thoughts of the ex had subsided for the moment. "Oh, I know! At lunch there was a little kid sitting at the table next to me, and he kept giggling at me and I was making faces at him. It was so cute!" She paused for a few seconds. "Oh, and my boss took our whole team out to lunch unexpectedly, for no reason. That was a really nice surprise!"

"Great! One more," I said.

"Um, let's see. I'm proud of myself that I got up early and went to the gym?" It was more a question than a statement.

"Well," I said, "I loved hearing the way you got excited about the first two. You're not as sure about the last one, and I'd love to hear about

something that just lights you up." I could tell her mind was going
blank for the moment, so I told her to text a third to me before she fell
asleep that night. She agreed and I asked what it was that she wanted
to vent about Bobby.

"You know, it's nothing," she said. "I was just in a spin, mad at him
again. But I feel better now, thinking about my day, so I don't really
want to go back to thinking about him now. I like this little game!
Thanks, Dina. I guess I just needed to get my mind off it for a sec. I'll
text you later!" And we hung up the phone.

Hours later, my phone buzzed with Kate's text: "Just got a call from
my dad. We had such a good talk. It made me smile inside."

I thought, *I think I like this better, a smile-inside list, rather than a
gratitude list. I just might start doing that myself!*

I had been making gratitude lists on and off for years, and had
noticed that they weren't always that effective. Sometimes when I'm
writing down what I'm grateful for, it's really a list of things that I feel
guilty about taking for granted—a nice place to live, plenty of food—
and it doesn't really make me feel any better to write it. But this…
this could be a lot more fun. I continued to be amazed at how much
helping Kate was helping me too.

Weeks went by and before we both knew it, Kate had been back
in sobriety for ninety days. We continued our regular talks and
meetings and she renewed her commitment to staying sober this
time around.

I was driving home from work one afternoon and my cell phone
buzzed on the seat next to me. Usually I turned my phone off while I
was in the car since driving had become a special meditation time for
me, but this time I had forgotten. Kate's name showed on the display.
She might just be calling to check in, but then again she might need
something. I picked up her call.

"Dina! Oh my gosh! Do you have time to talk?" she asked excitedly.

"Yes, yes, of course," I responded as I pulled my car over to park at a curb. I wanted to give her my undivided attention.

"Dina! I haven't had a cigarette in two weeks! I hadn't even noticed that I wasn't smoking until just now!"

I was genuinely surprised by this. Kate had been a casual smoker during her drinking-and-drugging career, but as soon as she got sober she became a heavy smoker. This isn't uncommon; when people quit an addiction, another often takes its place. For me it was food; for Kate, tobacco.

"How in the world could you have not noticed you weren't smoking?" I asked in amazement.

"Well, usually at work I go outside for a smoke break a couple times a day with the same people. I'd been doing that, but the week before last, I felt like I was coming down with a cold, so I didn't have the desire to smoke. It's weird but whenever I feel under the weather, my craving for a cigarette goes out the window.

"Anyway, I didn't give much thought to it, but I never did come down with the cold and I got a lot of rest over that weekend. The following Monday I was back at work, and I headed out for my smoke break and lit a cigarette out of habit. As I went to take a drag off it, I totally stopped myself because I realized I hadn't had one in four days!

"Then, the past week and a half I've been going out for my usual smoke break, lighting one and immediately putting it out. I keep thinking the craving will come back, and since I didn't get sick, my desire to smoke will come back. But it hasn't! And it's been two weeks!"

"I can't believe it! So are you craving a smoke now?" I asked her.

"Nope! I didn't even take a drag off the one earlier today and the craving isn't there right now. I'm sure I could pick it back up easily if I wanted to, but since I don't want to, I'm rolling with it!"

I laughed in delight. "Why do you think the craving is gone?" I asked.

"Well, I don't really know. But this past week my meditations have been really great. I've been feeling so good, so close to God, so centered. It's the best I've felt in a good long time. It's like the craving to smoke has been lifted just like the craving to drink was. It's not even hard. I just don't want it right now!"

I was amazed at this and so happy for her. "Kate, you need to write a book called *How to Get Smoking to Quit You!*" I told her. "And I've been having a similar experience with food." I told her about how I'd been tuning in to what my body wanted before I ate anything.

"And Dina, one more thing. I know you said you've been driving with the radio off lately. Well I've been trying that too, and I had the most awesome experience today. I drove the same route I always do but it was somehow different. The trees looked like Disneyland trees. They were glowing and just so alive!"

I was completely surprised—no one else had ever understood what I'd meant by Disneyland trees, and I hadn't even told Kate about them because I didn't want her to think her coach was crazy. And yet here she was telling me her identical experience and using the same words I'd used to describe them. I was utterly amazed at the coincidence.

"One of the suggestions you gave me for my 3x3 has really been working for me this week," Kate said. "I wonder if it has anything to do with it. In every meditation I've been saying, 'I'm open; I'm willing; just show me.' I've been feeling so receptive to listening to my intuition, and I like the way I feel. It's like nothing is a big deal; everything will be okay. Nothing has control over me right now. It feels so freeing!"

I had forgotten that I'd shared that little mantra with her. It's the one I used whenever I was feeling overwhelmed. "Amazing, Kate! That is so inspiring! I'm so happy for you!"

"Me too, Dina, I just feel so good. I'll see you this weekend!"

"See you then." I smiled. *How fantastic that I get to have this woman in my life*, I thought as I shut off my phone and pulled back out onto the road, heading home. I felt so lucky. So very, very lucky.

chapter twelve

healing from
addiction

"Truth is whatever is subjectively convincing at one's
current level of perception."
— David R. Hawkins, M.D., Ph.D.

J esse and I kept up our routine of going for walks every
Saturday morning in the following months. My work with
her almost immediately went far beyond the bounds of the
recovery program. She was one of the few people I confided in about
my experiences in higher consciousness. No one else I talked to at
the recovery center (or anywhere else in my life, for that matter)
was experiencing anything remotely like what was happening
within me.

No one talked of giggling trees and—would you believe?—they looked at me a little funny when I did. But Jesse was different; she'd actually had similar experiences and knew that, even though these blissful states of being were rare and elusive, they were much more real than our usual, everyday perspective.

Several months into working with Jesse, I was consistently having experiences of higher awareness at the recovery center meetings. One day I was sitting in a group at the center in that blissful state, and it occurred to me, plain as day, that there was a level of healing from addiction that was far beyond what we were experiencing in the program, or even believed was possible.

I had the idea that it's possible to heal anything and everything about our bodies, including addiction. It wasn't a "what if" thought. From that perspective of higher consciousness, it was obvious to me that my body is just a physical manifestation of my thoughts, and if I truly believed that complete healing from addiction was possible, my body would conform to that belief.

At first when these ideas occurred to me, warning bells went off in my head. *Who are you trying to kid?* my mind chided. *Who do you think you are, entertaining the idea that an alcoholic could ever safely drink again, and why would you even want to? Don't you know these thoughts are just your addiction trying to lure you back?* After all, wasn't I the same person who less than two years earlier had thought that she could control her drinking? And that abstaining altogether was an overkill solution? The same girl who had hit the lowest low of her life after testing that very theory?

But as my time spent in higher consciousness increased, I knew that the ideas I was intuiting were coming from a much different place than where I had been two years earlier. Back then, I was desperately grasping at any possibility that would keep alcohol in my life. I was scared to death of losing access to the only thing that could soothe my depression and make me feel comfortable in my own skin. From where I was now, though, I had no need for alcohol as a self-soother. These new ideas of healing the body through the power of thought were on a whole different plane.

The possibility seemed ground-breaking and amazing, but I needed to talk to someone about it, and I knew it had to be Jesse. She and I had become very close and I trusted her completely. We were still taking our Saturday walks, so when the next one rolled around, I started talking as soon as our feet hit the pavement. "Jesse, this may surprise you since I've never mentioned it before, but I've been having these intense ideas of healing from addiction when I've been in states of higher consciousness." I walked her through everything I'd been thinking about and she just listened.

Then I said, "I'm not out to return to my old drinking habits of partying on weekends or having wine with dinner every night because an occasional drink is better than no drink at all. For me, this isn't about a former alcoholic becoming a normal drinker, this is about discovering the true capacity of my mind and spirit to heal my body from any sickness—even the demon that led me to want to end my own life.

"And what's most interesting to me," I continued, "is that these ideas never occur to me when I'm just going about my day. It's always been when I'm in a heightened state of awareness in meditation. And when these ideas come, it isn't even a question; it's plain as day that it's totally possible."

Jesse was quiet for a few moments, digesting all I had said. Then she said, "I remember you telling me about your healings in the past, and I've shared with you a few of my own. But I've always thought of addiction as something different. So tell me a little about how the healings you've experienced before relate to healing from addiction."

"Well," I said, "when I was younger I used to get strep throat a few times a year, and I always believed that the way to cure it was by using medicine, like everyone else does. And then, one year, I made the decision that I would never come down with it again—and I never have! I learned from that experience that anything physical starts out mental first. As soon as I began to believe that strep throat was a thing of the past and that my body knew how to stay healthy, that's what happened—I stayed healthy.

"So, the medicine was always effective, but what if it was the 'hard way' to go about healing? What if a much more natural and less invasive way of healing—that is, using the power of our thoughts and beliefs—is equally, if not more, effective?"

I took a breath and went on. "And there's another example. In the past few months I've completely changed the way I think about eating, and just from changing my mindset, my body has become leaner, healthier and more full of energy. I never used to be able to eat sugar in moderation, but now I just follow my intuition, and I've naturally lost my intense craving for it, without even consciously trying to. From this perspective I have total freedom; there are no foods that I can't have. I'm not counting calories; I'm just following my body's intuition. The only discipline I'm using is keeping up with my 3x3s."

Jesse listened intently as I continued.

"So I've seen from my experience that my body conforms to the thoughts I think about it, and there's no danger of falling into my old bingeing behaviors if I follow my intuition as to what to eat. And lately, what I'm sensing from the perspective of higher consciousness is that it's totally possible to regard alcohol in the same way—following my intuition alone on how much and when to have a drink."

I glanced over at Jesse as I finished. I was so curious to hear how she would respond.

"Wow this is really interesting, Dina," she said. "Now, you know I believe anything is possible, especially when we're in tune with our highest self. This possibility you're describing has never occurred to me, but I take it quite seriously since the idea only came to you when you were in heightened awareness. I've also heard extraordinary stories of people healing cancer and a whole gamut of ailments through their faith and belief alone. I just haven't heard about anyone healing an alcohol addiction that way."

Jesse continued to muse out loud. "But then, alcohol itself isn't the problem in the addiction—it's the *solution*. The problem is horrific disconnection from your innermost self—what you call the Big Me. People just drink to ease the pain of that disconnection. But what if that connection is restored and we no longer need the solution? Then what? How would our bodies react if we were to drink again?"

I jumped in. "All of this is exactly what's been rolling around in my mind the past couple of weeks. I wonder if anyone has ever had the experience of a full healing from addiction before?"

"There are lots of books and stories of self-healing," Jesse said. "Maybe if you search around online you might find something that resonates."

Of course! I needed to do some research. I promised to keep Jesse posted on my findings and headed home to see if I could find anyone else with experiences like mine.

—

Home from our walk, I started looking for books by others who had experienced self-healing, as well as doctors or scientists who have documented the power of thoughts and belief to heal the body. One of the first books I found on my search was titled *Biology of Belief: Unleashing the Power of Consciousness, Matter and Miracles*, by Bruce H. Lipton, Ph.D. This book made the hairs on my arms stand on end as I read it.

A few lines from the introduction hooked me immediately: "...we need to put Spirit back into the equation when we want to improve our physical and our mental health... It is not gene-directed hormones and neurotransmitters that control our bodies and our minds; our beliefs control our bodies, our minds, and thus our lives... When we cross that line and truly understand the New Biology, we will no longer fractiously debate the role of nurture and nature because we will realize that the fully conscious mind trumps both nature and nurture."

I was amazed to read that Dr. Lipton's research shows that the cells of our bodies, and literally our DNA, can be altered most directly through the deliberate focus of our thoughts. Past conditions, diagnoses and environments don't keep a hold over our minds and bodies once the fully conscious mind is engaged, but it's so rare that heightened consciousness is engaged that very few people even believe it's possible.

This emerging science, known as "epigenetics," shows that markers within our DNA can be switched "on" or "off" throughout our lives, based on our beliefs. This blew my mind because I'd always thought that our DNA was the ultimate and unchanging authority on the biology of our bodies.

Dr. Lipton's book raised endless questions in my mind. I wondered, *What if our attitudes, choices and beliefs are causing both our illnesses and our healing experiences? How much physical healing can be explained by the power of the mind's intention, and what are the limits of this power? Can permanent healing of diseases be achieved simply by focusing the mind more effectively?*

Everything I was learning was amazing and exciting. I couldn't wait to talk it all over with Jesse.

When Jesse and I went for our walk the following Saturday, I told her about Dr. Lipton's research showing that our bodies, and literally our DNA, can be altered by our thoughts and emotions.

"This is just amazing, Dina!" Jesse exclaimed. "It doesn't surprise me one bit that science is finding that the cells of our bodies are directly influenced by our thoughts and emotions; I've long known that from my own personal experience. And after reflecting on our last conversation all week, I believe it's true even to the point of healing addiction."

A thought occurred to me. Impulsively, I said, "I hope you don't feel awkward, having been my coach within the recovery program, and now I'm branching out into all of this."

"I'm not uncomfortable at all!" Jesse replied. "I love to hear about your experiences. We can just maintain a friendship, rather than a mentorship." She took my hand. "You need to follow your intuition on this journey, Dina. I would never discourage you from that. I'm glad to be part of this exciting time for you. I'm happy to keep our walks every week, and we can talk about everything as it comes up for you."

After we finished up our walk that day, I headed home feeling very grateful to have the support of someone who understood me so completely.

Nothing much changed over the next few months; Jesse and I still met weekly and I kept searching out books and people who had had experiences with and explanations for self-healing. I even started reading about quantum physics. I didn't have the science background to understand a lot of it, but I felt it might hold some clues as to the nature of the connection between mind, body and belief.

During periods of higher awareness I continued to sense the very real possibility of eliminating addiction from my body. I spent many of my 3x3s visualizing one glass of wine being way too big to finish, or preferring iced tea over alcohol when I was free to choose between both. About eight months after I'd first intuited the idea that my alcohol addiction could be healed, I knew that I was ready to see if my body would react differently now when I drank alcohol.

As I had done in meditation before I talked with my old boss about the money I stole, I reached a point where I had no resistance to whatever might happen. Even if something went terribly wrong and I needed to start back at square one in the recovery program, I was completely willing to do that.

I'd been planning to have dinner with a good friend the following week, so I spent my meditations visualizing myself knowing intuitively whether or not to have a drink with dinner. My friend knew my story of the past couple of years, and I'd explained to her what I was doing, so when she offered me a glass of wine that night, I knew I would be safe with her if anything bad happened.

My friend wasn't worried. "I trust you completely," she said, "and more than that, I trust your connection to your higher power. If you believe you're safe, then I believe you're safe."

When the moment came, I accepted a glass of wine from her. I was planning to let myself have as much wine as I wanted—following only my intuition on how much to drink, rather than planning out the amount ahead of time—but I didn't even finish the glass. I didn't have a desire for more than that. Back when alcohol was my medicine and I was sick emotionally, I couldn't get enough. But now, drinking was like taking flu medicine when I didn't have the flu. The medicine isn't appealing if there are no symptoms to eradicate. No cravings woke up inside of me, and certainly no raging tiger. I was relieved to find that the whole experience was kind of anticlimactic.

For the next six months, I consciously maintained my focus on the belief that my body was completely healed from addiction and that alcohol was something I could take or leave. During those six months, I had wine with dinner once a week or so and never had the craving return. It's now been over a year since I first reintroduced alcohol into my body, and over the past six months I've drunk even less than I did the first six months. I've found that if I start to feel even a slight buzz from alcohol, I don't have the desire to continue drinking because that buzz clouds the mental clarity I have now and dulls the connection to my Big Me. It actually makes me feel worse than normal, not better.

In my years of addiction, I was always chasing peace and centeredness, desperately trying to fill a bottomless void. The peace I live with now is much deeper and infinitely more satisfying than my best alcohol high ever was. I found the freedom to drink alcohol in the same way I found freedom around food—by relying on my intuitive sense to guide me every step of the way.

And this made me wonder what else I could heal within my body.

chapter thirteen

my healing
continues

"For those who believe, no proof is necessary. For those who don't believe, no proof is possible."

— Stuart Chase

few months into my experience of healing from addiction, and almost two years after I'd developed the intuitive eating technique I shared in Chapter 7, it occurred to me that, if my 3x3 meditation could be so effective at ending cravings and addiction, it might also be able to even out imbalances in the cholesterol levels in my blood. Ever since I'd tried the high protein diets years earlier in my life, my overall cholesterol level had been higher than normal. Could my 3x3 meditations bring it to normal?

I was on an eight-day personal development retreat called "Breakthrough to Success" led by Jack Canfield in Arizona during the summer of 2011 when I started developing a 3x3 meditation specifically focused on my cholesterol levels. Throughout the retreat Jack led us through guided meditations, and they gave me the idea that I could visualize the blood within my body healing and transforming during my 3x3 meditations. Plus, I was already scheduled for my annual blood work about two weeks after the retreat, which would give me a chance to see the results.

After a few days of trying different visualizations during my 3x3, I found one that I liked best. I started out visualizing a gentle but laser-like beam of healing energy entering my body straight into my heart. I imagined a warm sensation as the beam infiltrated and surrounded my heart. As the warmth grew stronger, I pictured the healing energy in the form of a thick liquid or serum, like warm honey, slowly seeping from my heart muscle into my bloodstream. I kept my focus on the warm feeling of the serum moving into my bloodstream in all directions. I followed it in my mind's eye, moving through my chest into my legs and arms, fingers and toes, and circling back again into my heart.

After a few of days of this specific focus in my 3x3 visualization, I could sense that my blood levels were evening out. I visualized the imaginary serum healing each blood cell it touched as it traveled throughout my body. After each three-minute meditation, I intuitively knew that my cholesterol levels were gradually bringing themselves back into balance.

Three weeks after the retreat, I had my routine blood work done as planned, and I was amazed, but at the same time not entirely surprised, by the results. My cholesterol was down from the prior year's reading of 227 to 177. I knew in my gut that the healing work I had done in meditation had caused the improvements, but it was still mind-blowing to realize the power of my belief and meditation to heal my own body.

I was seeing the power of the mind over the body more and more from my own experience, and my thoughts constantly went back to Dr. Lipton's book and his discussion of the science behind why and how the mind can so efficiently and dramatically improve the body. I wondered what comments Dr. Lipton would have on my own experience. Would he agree with the interpretations I had of his science; that is, that even in cases of addiction, belief can heal the body? Would he think I was crazy to even have tried it?

One afternoon, on impulse I sat down and wrote Dr. Lipton an email saying that I was writing a book about my healing experiences and requesting a phone interview with him to include in this book. I couldn't believe it when I got an email from his assistant telling me that he would be happy to spend half an hour on the phone with me! We set a date and I put together a list of questions that his book had inspired me to ask about my own healings.

I was nervous as the day of our phone interview approached, but it turned out to be a fun and enlightening experience. Dr. Lipton immediately made me feel at ease by asking me to call him Bruce, and I wasted no time in sharing my experiences and asking for his feedback. We ended up talking for over an hour.

I asked Bruce question after question about his theories and the specifics of my healings. My first question was, straight up, "I've spent three minutes three times a day in meditation for the past couple of years, and, even though three years ago I was a suicidal alcoholic, I've been able to drink alcohol since overcoming my addiction without having any cravings or negative side effects. Does that surprise you? Do you have any ideas that might explain my ability to do that?"

Bruce responded with a good-natured laugh and said that this didn't surprise him at all.

"The addiction isn't an illness, Dina," he told me. "It's not a physical, organic thing. The addiction is a consequence of learned experience and repetitions of patterns. Is alcoholism in the genes?" he asked me rhetorically. "The answer is no. In the science of epigenetics it's been found that it's the perception of your environment that controls your genes. You're not a victim of your genes because you're the one who can change your environment—or, more importantly, change your perception of your environment—and thus change your response to it."

I was excited to hear him say that my perceptions were the trumping factor, that by changing my perceptions (which I'd been doing with my 3x3s) I was changing my body.

"Let me tell you some fundamentals of how the mind works so this will be more clear to you," Bruce said. "The cells of your body are merely following instructions given by the nervous system, by the brain. The nervous system does the interpretation. You can easily see this when you see two people reacting to the same stimulus with very different reactions, one positive and one negative. As your perception changes, you change the message that your nervous system communicates to the cells of your body. Your mind controls your biology. That's what the placebo effect is about; the mind believes the pill will work and so it does."

Bruce continued. "Now, there are two different parts to the mind, the subconscious part and the conscious part. The subconscious is like a tape recorder, just playing old programs and running 95% of your reactions and decisions. For most people the conscious mind only operates about 5% of the time.

"In your case," he said, "with your three-minute, three-times-per-day meditations, you broke the norm. Those meditations constantly and consistently interrupted the tapes that the subconscious was playing. Your old tapes of needing a drink or feeling overwhelmed or frustrated or depressed in your life were constantly being run off their tracks. Even your belief, your subconscious tape, of defining yourself as an alcoholic and therefore never able to drink again, was interrupted. Without knowing it, you were doing one of the most powerful things you could have done in your own healing. You stopped listening to the subconscious tapes and started living in the present moment, in effect bringing yourself to your healing."

While I knew how effective my 3x3s were, I didn't really understand why until Bruce explained this to me. I had thought their value came from introducing positive ideas on a consistent basis. It was interesting to learn that their value was also in the regular interrupting of my old thought patterns, making it easier to leave them behind. I was so excited to have it put into a scientific context, and explained in language I could understand.

But I had a question. I asked Bruce, "I know 3x3 meditation has worked for me; do you think it could work to help others find their own healing too?"

Bruce said, "Well, I want to be clear that merely reading your book—or any self-help book—and being able to comprehend the concepts does not provide what's necessary for someone's subconscious to be rewired, for a reader to achieve their own healing. Understanding the concept is very different from integrating it into everyday life. It's *only* in constantly interrupting the tapes, or through an extraordinary experience like a deep, emotional transformative moment or a powerful hypnosis like you found in your 3x3 meditations that you can achieve self-healing. It's not hard to do, but it's not something that most people have experienced. It involves trusting the intuitive knowledge and letting go of the story playing subconsciously, which most people base their life decisions on without realizing it."

I was struck by his mention of hypnosis. I'd never done hypnosis before and was always a little skeptical of it, actually. But his description of it as achieving an open, receptive state of mind necessary for transformation, fit exactly with my experience in my 3x3s.

Another thought occurred to me. "I have an idea I'd like to run by you," I said. "It seems to me that the more centered I am within myself, the closer I am to my own source of well-being, and the closer I am to the power of healing. It's like there's a continuum of connection that underlies my life, and as I maintain my focus on staying connected to that power source, I feel happier and more fulfilled, and my body naturally stays healthier and free of addiction and disease. I'm coming to believe that sickness isn't unpredictable or random; it's just an indicator or symptom of how far I've wandered from my point of strongest connection. So the more connected I become, the more disease and addiction naturally fade from my body. And the more disconnected I am, the more sickness I experience. What do you think about that?"

"Absolutely," Bruce said. "The physical expression is the consequence of the mind's program—the program comes first, the physical expression second. The function of the mind is to create coherence between your beliefs and your reality."

I'd been following everything he said so far, but I got a little stuck on that last point. "Sorry, Bruce, but I didn't quite get that. Can you say more about it?"

"Of course!" Bruce said enthusiastically. "Meaning, if I have a belief, then the function of the mind is to manifest that belief so it becomes reality. For example, if I have a belief that I'm going to die of a disease because someone told me so, then the function of the mind is to convert that belief into physical manifestation, and it's no surprise that my belief becomes reality. But it's not because I have a terminal disease that I end up dying; it's because I *believe* this disease will kill me.

"Emotion is a telling factor," he continued. "If you have a strong emotion, positive or negative, around a certain belief, it pretty much ensures that the particular belief will become your physical reality. The science of epigenetics is not the science of being defined by your genes or environment; it's the science of understanding how your interpretation of your life events and environment affects the cells of your physical body."

All of this made perfect sense to me. As my beliefs about my body's ability to heal itself had changed, my body had changed. And it was the strong emotion connected to that ability—my passionate desire and deep knowing that I could have complete freedom from addiction and disease—that ensured that this became my reality.

Bruce ended our conversation with words that summed up the crux of what I had learned about healing since beginning my 3x3 practice.

"The important thing is to be present, as they say in Buddhism," he said. "Being present is having your focus on the conscious mind, which breaks the cycle of what's being run by the subconscious mind. What you're doing in your 3x3 meditations is getting present. You're interrupting the old tape of negative beliefs and becoming intensely present, which is why you were able to experience what you've described as experiences in higher consciousness."

I especially loved his closing words: "Being fully present means not having a negative interpretation of what is happening in the moment; it's being an unbiased observer of it. You're free of your subconscious tapes in moments where you might have normally reacted differently, but your interpretation—and response—has started to change."

We ended the call with words of mutual appreciation, and I hung up the phone and sat for a few moments in silence, reflecting on everything I'd just learned. Bruce had explained more than

I'd even hoped for. He had explanations and a scientific context where I had only had first-hand experiences, and that expanded my understanding profoundly.

———

As Bruce said to me during our chat, just reading this book—or any book—isn't enough to cause transformation. Everyone has their own best path and their own truth that they need to follow. I've shared my story and Bruce's knowledge here, hoping to give anyone who has experienced less than optimum health and well-being the inspiration and hope that, no matter how bad the affliction has been, our thoughts and beliefs can be changed with practice and discipline.

That means the possibility for healing is always there. I believe that the starting place of all healing is the trust and commitment to follow our inner guidance, those internal nudges, and maintain an open mind to think very differently than we have in the past.

For those struggling with addiction, I wouldn't advise you to start out where I finished. Recovery and healing is a process that needs to start at the beginning. The addiction recovery center I began this journey with literally saved my life, and I'd encourage anyone wrestling with addiction to call a local recovery program. And look to harness the power of meditation, intuition and visualization to increase your connection to your higher power, your source of well-being. That connection is what will provide healing from addiction and other sicknesses.

Of course, everyone has a unique path to follow. I never expected my path to take the turns it did, and I offer my story as just one example among thousands of possible journeys to healing and wellness.

If you have resonated with my experiences so far, you might find Part II helpful as well. There, I offer further suggestions and details regarding the use of the techniques I've found to be effective. I hope you will enjoy them and also discover others that may suit you even better. Once we start tuning into our inner guidance and really listening to it, an infinite number of new techniques could be illuminated. There is so much to learn as we shift to an intuitive understanding of our bodies, our minds and our lives.

part two

your turn

introduction
to the games

"Training your mind is what it all boils down to. All of it. All things. Everything. 'Todo.'"

— Mike Dooley

i want you to have something concrete to take away from this book, so the next few pages will detail some of the processes—or "games," as I call them—that have worked for me in my personal transformation.

The easiest way for me to take a new idea and see how it works or doesn't work is to make a game out of it. Playing one of these games means that I will keep a flicker of awareness in the back of my mind all day long, watching out for or prioritizing whatever I do that day in line with the rules of that day's game. I only commit to playing a game for seven days at a time because I've found I'm more likely to keep my commitment if it's only for a week. After every seven days, I renew my

135

commitment to the same game or choose a new game for the following week. The foundation of all these games is the 3x3 meditation.

Some of these games have been fully detailed in earlier chapters so you can go back and refer to them there; some didn't get a mention or enough detail. Other games I developed through coaching others rather than from my own experience. So this section includes a review of some games and an introduction to others.

In his book *The Success Principles: How to Get From Where You Are to Where You Want to Be*, Jack Canfield brilliantly sums up the benefit I've gotten from using these games to change my perspective:

> Imagine that you suddenly discovered you were driving with the emergency brake on. Would you push harder on the gas? No! You would simply release the brake and instantly go faster—without any additional expenditure of energy. Most of us are going through life with the emergency brake on. It's time to release the limiting beliefs, emotional blocks, and self-destructive behaviors that are holding you back.

Don't you wonder why sometimes you feel like you're in a great groove (or "the zone" as I've heard it referred to), getting three weeks' worth of work done in two days? And other times it's a struggle just to do the minimum? It seems like these grooves are random and unexpected, or lucky. Not so. You can get in the habit of tuning in and letting the groove become a more and more regular part of your experience. That's one of the major benefits I've gotten from these games.

People I've shared these games with have come up with their own twists on them too. I've played them the way I've written them here, but one size doesn't fit all. I don't believe we are here to all come to an agreement on a few ideas and find the one right, true path. We are here to use our minds and imaginations to create better lives for ourselves and those around us. You may come up with your own twist on a game that works much better for you than the way I've outlined it here. It's more important to follow the promptings of your own intuition than it is to follow the steps exactly.

I invite you to use these games in whatever ways they are most effective for you, consulting with a mentor, coach or health professional, if appropriate, before you begin. I hope these games bring you the joy and freedom they have brought me.

game one

the 3 x 3

"Meditation is a way to raise the energy of Life that is always present in your body."
— **Neale Donald Walsch**

I hardly ever spend more than three-minutes, three times a day in meditation. The way that I've spent these short bursts of time has gradually changed my attitude toward just about everyone and everything in my life, bringing me little by little to centeredness and freedom.

If you have a daily meditation practice you like, by all means stay with that. But if you haven't been able to stick with any practice you've tried or you haven't felt it was effective, you might like to try the 3x3. I think even just 30 seconds of true, uninterrupted inner quiet is better than ten minutes of peeking through closed eyes at the clock, or mentally making your grocery list, while hoping to achieve enlightenment.

Connecting inwardly multiple times a day has the advantage over one long meditation of shifting your mindset continuously, and repeatedly reminding you of what's important throughout the day. Sometimes I don't want to stop after three minutes and continue to meditate peacefully for 15–20 minutes. But even if I do that, I still make sure I sit for the other two 3x3s that day. The daily goal isn't to meditate for nine or more minutes in total; the goal is to find that inner calm several times throughout the day.

What you get in meditation is access to power that is far beyond the limits of your thinking mind. Some people call it God, or Source Energy, or their Inner Being, or simply higher consciousness. One woman I've coached thinks of it as re-charging her batteries several times a day. She pictures a power cord extending from her heart that she can plug into an invisible outlet above her body. If the cord is not securely plugged in, or has fallen out completely, she loses her sense of centeredness, of peace and connection. That's when she finds herself looking for ways to access power outside herself (trying to plug her power cord into food or alcohol or other people), even though there's only one true outlet her power cord was designed for.

The same thing happens to me sometimes. When I'm disconnected, it shows up in many small ways. Sometimes I find myself mentally putting others down in subtle ways that make me feel better about myself. I've found myself becoming needy with guys I've dated, and more irritable if little things go wrong. When I attempt to recharge my batteries by trying to get people to do what I think I need them to do, or treat me the way I want them to, what I'm really doing is trying to plug my power cord into different people or situations and demanding that they be the source of energy that recharges my batteries.

But nothing outside of my innermost essence (or God or Source Energy) was designed to supply me with the power that I need, and so it never works. When I find myself doing any of these things, I try to catch myself and see the impulse for what it is: simply a symptom that my batteries are low and I need to plug in to the only source that can give me power. And I do that in my 3x3 meditations.

There are a few different ways that I structure my 3x3s:

1. Many times I will do nothing more than sit quietly with my eyes closed and count how many times my heart beats during the three minutes. When I first started meditating, I tried counting how many breaths I took but kept getting distracted—maybe because there was so much time between breaths that my mind had a chance to wander. For whatever reason, putting a hand over my chest to feel and count my heartbeats with my eyes closed keeps me completely focused. Even if my thoughts are negative or overwhelming before I sit down to meditate, distracting myself with this little task always gives me relief.

2. It also helps for me to have a mantra or some words I can repeat over and over to give my crazy mind something to put its focus on. My favorite mantra that I use when I'm feeling overwhelmed, anxious or paralyzed with fear is: "I'm open. I'm willing. Show me. Guide me from within." This mantra puts space around whatever thoughts are choking me and creates an opening inside of me for willingness, letting go and a bit of peace. You can choose whatever words suit you. Other examples are:

    a. "I know there is another way to approach this. Just because I can't see it right now doesn't mean it's not there.

I am open to the possibility of a new idea, a new way of doing this."

b. "There is space inside me for new ideas to flow in and to show themselves. I don't have all the answers and I don't need to. I'm open to new ideas."

It doesn't matter if you are praying these words to God or simply putting forth your intention to try to clear a path to access the inner intuitive voice. Either way, it works for me and it has worked for others who have very different ideas of God than I do.

3. I also use my 3x3 in preparation for conversations with other people or to get ready to do tasks I really dread, or to change anything in my life that is not going the way I would like. In these situations I use visualization to address the situation as it is and make peace with it or replace it with a more ideal situation.

In every 3x3 my fundamental intention is to connect with my intuition. I am being alert to the inner voice, or nudge, of guidance that can come only in the silence. This is the source of all transformation, and the first step to the solution to all problems, in my experience. Thus, many of the other games rely on this fundamental 3x3 practice.

Once you're comfortable in your 3x3 and you can feel yourself shift into a more mellow, focused state during your meditations, try to tap back into that state at different times throughout your day. Just for a couple of minutes here and there. I first tried it during my pre-meeting conversations with new friends at the recovery center. The conversations were usually less than five minutes long, and they were a pleasant thing for me to do, so it was relatively easy to be in that state at the same time. Maintaining that state of inner calm while interacting with others or doing another activity is the next step after being able to find that space within during the 3x3.

I can also access this inner space very successfully while taking walks. I used to think walks were boring and pointless. *I'm already here at home,* I used to think, *why would I leave and walk around the block just to come right back here again?* But the point is the walk itself, not where you're going. Even a five- or ten-minute mindful walk around the block can shift your mood.

The whole point is to be able to be as peaceful and non-resistant in your real life as you are in meditation, by trying it a few minutes at a time.

game two

w a t c h y o u r s e l f

"There is nothing either good or bad, but thinking makes it so."

— William Shakespeare

Watch Yourself is a game that developed out of my experiences coaching others, so there aren't any examples from my own life in this description. It's most effective for people who are in a generally good frame of mind but stuck in one or two areas of their life. This game can give you insight into what exactly is keeping you stuck.

You may already be familiar with the Law of Attraction, which states that "like attracts like," especially when it comes to thoughts in your mind. This means our minds attract or come up with more thoughts like the ones that we habitually think. The point of this game is to shed light on what's keeping you stuck (that is, which thoughts or topics tend to bring you into a negative tailspin, inundated by more and more negative thoughts) and to remind you to turn your thinking around once you notice what's happening. It's much harder to change a behavior that you're not aware of, so increasing your awareness is the first step.

This game, like most of these games, is played for seven days. Playing this game for seven days once every few weeks is ideal for maintaining awareness of your thoughts. I don't encourage people to play it for more than two weeks in a row because after that length of time you should have enough notes to be able to see your patterns of thought, and that's all you really need.

DAY ONE

1. During your 3x3s focus on maintaining awareness of your thoughts throughout the day, rather than just letting them go on by themselves as they normally do. Eckhart Tolle calls this "the watcher" within ourselves. The priority is simply to watch your thoughts without engaging in them, as if you were a separate person observing them.

2. Write down a quick note whenever you catch a negative thought that day (I'm fat; I'm ugly; I can't do this; this isn't worth it; I'll never get it right; she's ugly; he's incompetent; what's wrong with the guy driving in front of me, etc.) Jot down a couple of words that will jog your memory of the negative thought when you review it later. Remember that your thoughts aren't *you,* and there's nothing abnormal about having a lot of negative thoughts. They're just a habit. After you spend this time becoming aware of the habit, you can then put your focus on changing it.

3. At the end of the day, look at your list. It doesn't matter if there are 20 things, 100 things or 1,000 things on it. Get a feel for a handful of recurring themes in your thoughts (I'm not worthy; everyone at work is incompetent; no one knows how to drive, etc.) and make a new list with just these themes. Note that the act of writing down each thought as you notice it and the act of writing down the themes later are both critical. Just noticing the thoughts or mentally listing them won't have nearly the impact of a clear-cut list. Writing is a focused exercise and the act of writing trains your ability to focus your inner watcher.

4. Determine a trump thought to switch to when you catch yourself in a mind-spin about any of the negative thoughts in the categories. This should be a positive thought that changes your gears, such as looking forward to an upcoming event or vacation or to going out to dinner tonight, or being excited about good news you've had.

DAYS TWO – SEVEN

1. During your 3x3s each day have the intention to be the watcher for the day—to observe yourself interacting with others and observe your thoughts in a non-judgmental way. (If you beat yourself up for thinking these thoughts instead, put those self-shaming thoughts on your list!)

2. Review your list of themes of negative thoughts (usually around 5–7) each day and notice when the themes pop up in your thoughts throughout the day.

3. As you catch yourself in your negative thoughts during the day, turn your attention immediately to your trump thought. It might not feel terrific in that moment to dwell on something that may seem far away or irrelevant, but the important

thing is that you're interrupting a habit. Just noticing it and interrupting it is enough.

Continue this practice for seven full days. After just a few days of playing this game diligently you will probably notice something shifting or opening or a sense of relief within you. At the end of Day Seven, decide if you want to renew and play again for another seven days. Only commit to seven days at a time.

game three

picture it first

"You draw into your life what you give attention to."
— Janet Bray Attwood and Chris Attwood

f or the most part, I don't do anything until I feel like doing it.
You'll remember this one from Chapter 5 when Jesse taught me to enjoy doing the laundry. Instead of putting my focus on enduring a task or thinking of how happy I'll be when I finally get it over with, I take the time to visualize enjoying the task itself. The visualization changes the way I look at the task and brings me to a place of being inspired from within to get it done.

For example, if I wanted to get into a workout routine, I wouldn't begin by forcing myself out of bed and off to the gym where I hate every second of my workout but do it anyway because I figure it's for my own good. This sheer willpower method might be an effective jumpstart for the first few days of a lifestyle change, but if I don't get to the point where I'm really enjoying working out, I will lose motivation after a short time and quit. This much I know from lots of experience.

So, instead of all that forcing, I visualize. For example, when I decided to start running at age 35 for the first time in my life, I didn't run at all for the first two weeks. I simply spent my 3x3 meditations visualizing suiting up in running clothes, choosing my music playlist, and jogging a short distance without getting out of breath. After two weeks my desire to actually go for a short jog was so strong I just went!

I started out slowly and joined a small group of women runners so I could get the techniques and everything right. I didn't push myself, and I kept my 3x3s consistent during my first several weeks of running. Before long, I had reached a point where I actually felt worse if I skipped going for a run than if I ran. Once I hit that point, the running took care of itself. Within two months of never having run in my life, I completed my first 5K race.

The point of the game is to visualize doing something until you are simply inspired to take the physical action. At that point you're no longer resisting the activity but actually looking forward to it.

Now, this game does not mean skipping out on things I've committed to, just because I don't feel like doing them. If I'm dreading something, like taking a test or giving a presentation, I visualize it going successfully, as if it's no big deal. Then when the time for the test or presentation comes around, even if I'm not jumping for joy over it, at least my dread and anxiety are significantly lessened. The key is to lower the inner attitude of resistance toward whatever you don't want to do.

This Picture It First game has helped neutralize my feelings of anxiety about pretty much anything I have to do, or I think I should do, but don't really want to do. And it's helped me to enjoy everyday errands I used to feel neutral about. I visualize chatting with friendly cashiers at the grocery store, finding everything I need in stock, actually remembering to bring my list with me, etc. I can be as detailed as I want to be in my visualizations. I get to the place where I can relax into the action rather than fight tooth and nail against doing it. This game has switched my attitude from enduring and tolerating my life to finding even the most mundane parts of my life fulfilling and enjoyable.

I've learned that you no longer need to motivate yourself to do something when you're naturally inspired to do it because you enjoy it. That's the gift of playing Picture It First.

game four

p r e - f o r g i v e n e s s

"How people treat you is their karma. How you react is yours."

— Dr. Wayne Dyer

re-forgiveness is the game I first played to prepare for interacting with Gary, the guy in my group of friends who used to get under my skin. For me, pre-forgiving means silently granting people all the space in the world to be, say or do whatever they want to be, say or do while I'm around them.

This little game developed out of my understanding that whenever I'm upset with someone, the problem is really not what the other person is doing, the problem is in the lens through which I am viewing their behavior. When I'm truly centered, the behaviors and actions of others kind of go through me; I feel free and light and transparent. It's the opposite of having a thick skin—it's removing any barrier between myself and others and maintaining my inner connection regardless of my circumstances and other people's behaviors.

I find this game to be so effective that at this point I look forward to interacting with people I find challenging because it "ups my game." Mentally preparing for the interaction puts me into a state of being totally present when it's taking place.

When I'm playing Pre-forgiveness, my mindset is that I am granting someone else permission to do something, so I have the feeling that I'm in control. I get the satisfaction of thinking I'm dictating what occurs in my reality! But what actually happens when you give people permission to do whatever they want is that you get the opposite of control. You get freedom. And that's a much, much better thing to have than control. Actually controlling someone is a lot of work—you're almost enslaved by monitoring whether or not they're doing what they're supposed to do. Giving others permission to do whatever they want to do gives you both freedom instead.

So Pre-forgiveness sets you up to feel empowered *and* free.

I play this game within my 3x3s in the days prior to the encounter. I often start with the thought, *What if this moment, this person, this experience, is perfect just the way it is? What if I can still be happy and free even if nothing changes?*

Then I visualize in three stages, starting with #1, below, in my first 3x3. If I don't reach the point in my visualization where I feel comfortable with it, I do it again in my next 3x3 until I do. Then I move on to #2 and #3, taking as many 3x3 meditations as I need.

Here are the stages:

1. Visualize not reacting to the person. (I'm keeping my reaction in check but feeling irritated.) This is the stage where I mentally gave Gary permission to be, say or do whatever he wants.

2. Visualize not even wanting to react. (I'm feeling neutral, not irritated.)
3. Visualize finding his behavior endearing (I'm thinking, *There he is, that old Gary, just doing that thing he always does when I see him!*)

When the time for the encounter comes, if you find yourself getting frustrated or angry or fearful before or during it, catch that thought, interrupt it and mentally re-gift the person the permission to be or say or do whatever he or she wants. Sometimes I do that a couple dozen times in the course of a day, in and out of my 3x3s. But notice that, when you do it consistently, you'll likely feel a little freer than usual. You may have more space around your thoughts, rather than your thoughts just being on auto-pilot. And the freedom from being at the mercy of our own thoughts, as well as the other person's behavior, is the goal.

game five

s m i l e - i n s i d e   l i s t

"When you are grateful, fear disappears and abundance appears."
— **Anthony Robbins,** World-renowned authority on psychology of leadership, negotiations, organizational turnaround and peak performance

My twist on the gratitude list is the Smile-inside List. It lifts my spirits as I try to remember points throughout my day or my week that made me laugh or feel good. These are times when I feel a genuine smile inside myself, and might have even smiled on the outside. It could be a beautiful garden I saw on my walk, or a child making faces at me across a restaurant, or a big sloppy kiss from a friend's dog. I recall the event in as much detail as I can to recreate that good feeling.

You can use a blank notebook or your journal for making your daily Smile-inside List. I usually write it at the end of my day, after dinner but well before bedtime because if I'm too tired I'm likely to skip it.

The only instruction is to write out three or four sentences describing each event and see if that doesn't shift the way you feel inside. If you don't immediately feel a shift, write a little more detail or choose a different event altogether. Here are a couple of examples of how I've switched from my idea of a gratitude list to a Smile-inside List:

Old way: "I'm grateful that I have enough to eat."

New way: "I had such a good time with my friend Martha at lunch today. I haven't laughed like that in a long time! The salad I ordered was more delicious than usual, and I felt really good about eating something healthy. Hearing Martha update me about her life and even helping her make a decision she's been struggling with was so satisfying. It was the highlight of my day!"

Old way: "I'm grateful that I still have a job in this economy."

New way: "That was the best team meeting we've had in a long time. When Georgia told us about how she's dressing up as our CEO for Halloween we laughed so hard. It's awesome that we're all getting along so well these days."

You can tell if you're capturing it well if you feel energized when you read back over your description. It might be a slow start at first, but once you get the hang of it, you'll see that this game can really shift your mood and attitude.

game six

who knew?

"If you are irritated by every rub, how will you be polished?"

— **Rumi**

his game helps me get unstuck from a belief that is paralyzing me. What gets me stuck in the first place is thinking that this belief is a fact.

For example, here are some beliefs that have paralyzed me in the past:

- "She doesn't like me; she's just being nice."
- "I'm so inefficient and I have way too much to do. I never get anything done on time!"

Who Knew has three steps:

1. Name a limiting belief that seems like a fact, something you believe will never change and is keeping you feeling overwhelmed or paralyzed.
2. Find evidence that weakens that belief. List at least three things that disprove or at least diminish the intensity of the paralyzing statement.
3. With someone else, or just in your 3x3 meditation, go over each thing you listed in Step Two, considering it fully and using it as leverage to get some breathing room around the limiting belief.

Here are a couple of examples:

STEP ONE:
I'm disorganized and I'm months behind in my personal paperwork. I will never get all of this done!

STEP TWO:
- I have felt like this before, and have been OK. I know that this feeling is temporary and that it will pass.
- I can't get everything done all at once anyway. What I can do is make a list of everything I need to get done and divide it into manageable portions. I know that if I focus on just one thing at a time the list will get done.
- Other people I know have felt like this too. I know that what I'm feeling is completely normal. Talking to my friend (counselor/sister/cat/etc.) about it has helped me put it into perspective in the past, and I'm willing to do that again.

STEP THREE:

Share what you've written with someone. Lots of times what's keeping us paralyzed is hiding our fears and insecurities. Unlock the closet and bring them into the light. Sharing alone may alleviate much of your anxiety. Bringing it into the 3x3 meditation is helpful too. Set your timer for three minutes and take a few slow, deep breaths. Consider each of the statements you wrote in Step Two silently. I usually conclude my meditation by asking inwardly, *I am open to new ideas. I am willing to try this a new way. I trust my intuition. Show me from within.*

Even if you don't end up doing cartwheels in excitement after this process, you will probably have a sense of relief and of putting the negative belief in perspective and getting some space around it. Little by little, as you continue to view your thoughts from a distance, they will consume you less and less. One by one, the negative beliefs that paralyzed you will lose their power over you.

Here is another example:

STEP ONE:

Food is my enemy. I hate my obsessive cravings and my chubby body!

STEP TWO:

- My body was designed to eat. I cannot change that. But it's not only possible, it's actually my default state to eat healthy foods and to feel comfortable in my body.
- Even though I can't see it right now, I know that finding balance and peace with food is possible and easier than I think.
- Maybe I am making this into too big of a deal. I do enjoy food, and I have felt physically vibrant in the past. If it's something

I've already done, it will be even easier to find it again this time around.

- I'm willing to approach food in a new way. I'm willing to try tuning in to my body's signals and eating according to them just for the next few days. I'll see how it goes and re-evaluate after that.

STEP THREE:

Same as above: share your thoughts with another. Bring the issue into your 3x3 and review each of the points. Notice how each one affects your feelings.

What we think is the problem usually isn't. I used to think that the tempting foods all around me were the problem, or that my sugar cravings were the problem, or the need to eat was the problem! But the problem isn't any of those things. The problem is our lack of connection with our own bodies, our emotional attachment to food, and our lack of fulfillment from within. Anything that gives us relief or space around the negative thoughts creates room for a new idea or perspective to take root and lets the light and wisdom between the thoughts shine through.

—

Please keep in mind that these games are just guidelines and that your intuition will always lead you in the direction that's best for you. My wish for you is that you find your own techniques that unlock access to your innermost self, and use others' suggestions (including mine!) only if those ideas resonate with your heart and your gut.

I have no doubt that following your own intuition will lead you to true happiness and peace in your life—possibly a lot faster than you could have imagined!

epilogue

It's now Summer 2012 and I'm ready to publish this book! So where am I now?

I've been steadily growing my life coaching business for the last year, after becoming a certified coach in April 2011. By December 2011 I was well enough along my path to leave my day job, and I've been traveling quite a bit around the country these last several months. I've been spending a lot more time with my family in New York and visiting friends and family in different cities since I can coach over Skype and write from pretty much anywhere. There is no question coaching others is my calling; nothing has ever uplifted or stretched me so much as when I'm helping others along their paths.

Jesse and I still walk together every week when I'm in California. Grace and Kate are still part of my life too; we stay in touch and share our milestones with each other. Though I don't coach Kate these days since I'm no longer in the recovery program, she's still a bright light in my life.

I've found myself drawn to reading books about quantum physics and about the links between science and spirituality, and stories of others who have healed their bodies and minds using meditation or other "inner" techniques. This completely different plane on which I've come to live my life—the plane of true freedom, true connection, and fullest self-expression—keeps me yearning to learn more and more about the how and why of life and the power of mini-meditation and visualization. And I'm yearning to meet others who have had similar experiences and those who understand and can explain why and how such simple techniques can transform everything.

My 3x3 meditations continue to expand as I keep having new life situations to gear them towards. I'll be sharing my ongoing learning experiences, insights and resources on my website, www.madlychasingpeace.com. I'd love if you'd keep in touch with me there.

Life today is better than I ever thought it could be. My days are full of joy in the simplest things.

And yes, I still love doing the laundry.

acknowledgments

It took a village to help me write this book and my heart is full of appreciation. In early 2010 I decided I wanted to get a hobby and was trying to decide between taking a class in Spanish, knitting or writing. I'm so glad I chose writing!

I want to thank Rachelle for being my first writing mentor, and Joy for being my first writing buddy. Without your encouragement I may never have started telling my story through the written word. Thank you.

To Peggy McColl, my mentor and my good friend. You inspire me, enlighten me, make me laugh, open my mind, warm my heart. I'm so grateful to have you in my life.

To Bruce Lipton, the first person who connected the dots for me so I could understand the link between spirituality and science. Thank you for your patience and passion in sharing your wisdom with me in a way I could truly understand.

To Jack Canfield, words cannot begin to express how much my life has changed since I met you and you read my raw, messy, unedited writings before they turned into this book. Your belief in me and my message skyrocketed me into becoming a coach and published author (and to having the faith to leave my day job!). I've had a major personal breakthrough every occasion I've spent time with you. You're my good luck charm.

To Patty Aubery, for your presence, your friendship, and sharing your beautiful spirit with me. The first time I met you I felt like I'd known you forever. Thank you for being so openly supportive of me.

To Cindy Buck, my patient, eagle-eyed editor. Your ideas have helped me tremendously in structuring this book, and your eye for detail will never cease to amaze me. Thank you for all you've done to polish this manuscript and for being a true friend to me.

To Carol Kline, for opening your home to me and sharing your insights on my writing and my message. Your intuitive writer's sense is a true gift and I feel honored that you've shared it with me.

To Janet Attwood, for having an infectious passion for life and sharing that openly with me. I love connecting with people like you who love to uplift others. I always feel like I can do anything when I'm around you.

To Amy Swift Crosby, for helping me find my writing voice. Your guidance as I struggled to piece my writings together into this book was invaluable. Thank you.

To Mary, my "accountabilibuddy," for believing in me, sharing this journey with me, and holding me accountable to my own goals. I'm always energized and inspired after our talks.

To my mastermind group: Jean, Melanie, Cindy and Blane. It's hard to find words to tell you how much I've come to adore and love you guys. There are times when I feel like my dreams are too big, but even when I doubt myself, you never, ever do. I don't know where I'd be without your unwavering support and friendship.

To Kari, my blogging buddy who I end up talking so much with that I haven't done my blog! Our talks uplift and inspire me in a way I can't explain; the way you draw the best from me and ask me questions I didn't know I knew the answer to is a gift I'm so blessed to benefit from.

To my parents and sisters, for being exactly who you are and loving me for exactly who I am. Sometimes the road gets rocky, but it always, always, always turns out for the best. I love you.

To Hersh, one of the people who knows me best on this planet. Thank you for your love and friendship and complete understanding and acceptance of me as I shared the hardest times of my life with you, long before I thought I'd be sharing them with the world.

To Grace, for being one of the two people I bared my soul to during the darkest days of my life. Thank you for always remaining steady and for your "tough love." I would not be the same person I am today without the foundation you helped me build in those early days. I will always feel connected to you no matter where our individual paths take us.

To Hank, for being the other person who held my hand during my darkest days. You made food for me and got me out of my house when I didn't have the ability to do those things for myself. I could never repay all you've given me.

To Kate, for being one of the brightest lights in my life. You always thanked me, but I'm quite sure I gained from you infinitely more than I was able to give. I love you unconditionally and adore watching the amazing woman you continue to become.

And finally, to Jesse, where to even start! I used to get so frustrated that you never left your joyous plane to join me in my rational thinking or to sympathize when I was wallowing in self-pity. If you hadn't stayed exactly who you were I never would have raised myself to meet you on that plane. Thank you, really, just for being you.

p e r m i s s i o n s
& c r e d i t s

Front cover font for the words *madly, hell,* and *happy* by John Bigsby
www.dollarafont.com

p xiii   Deepak Chopra quote excerpted from *How to Know God* 2006
DVD. www.deepakchopra.com

p 25   Eckhart Tolle quote excerpted from *The Power of Now* Copyright
© 1997 by Eckhart Tolle. Reprinted with permission from
New World Library, Novato, CA. www.newworldlibrary.com

p 71   Abraham-Hicks quote excerpted from the Abraham-Hicks
workshop in Silver Spring, MD on Saturday, May 11th,
2002, © by Jerry & Esther Hicks (830) 755-2299. www.
AbrahamHicks.com

p 105   Michael Bernard Beckwith quote excerpted from *Spiritual
Liberation: Fulfilling Your Soul's Potential* by Michael Bernard
Beckwith. Reprinted with permission. www.agapelive.com

p 113   David R. Hawkins quote excerpted from *Power vs. Force:
The Hidden Determinants of Human Behavior* by David R.
Hawkins, M.D., Ph.D. Reprinted with permission from
Veritas Publishing. www.veritaspub.com

p 118   Quoted text excerpted from *Biology of Belief: Unleashing the Power of Consciousness, Matter and Miracles*, by Bruce H. Lipton, Ph.D. Reprinted with permission from Bruce H. Lipton. www.brucelipton.com

p 135   © Mike Dooley quote from *A Note from the Universe*. Reprinted with permission. www.tut.com

p 136   Quoted text excerpted from *The Success Principles: How to Get From Where You Are to Where You Want to Be* by Jack Canfield with Janet Switzer. Reprinted with permission from Jack Canfield. www.thesuccessprinciples.com

p 145   William Shakespeare quote excerpted from *Hamlet*

p 149   Janet Bray Attwood and Chris Attwood quote excerpted from *The Passion Test: The Effortless Path to Discovering Your Life Purpose*. Reprinted with permission from Janet Bray Attwood. www.thepassiontest.com

p 157   Tony Robbins quote reprinted with permission from Robbins Research International, Inc. For more information, go to www.tonyrobbins.com

p 173   Dr. John Demartini quote excerpted from *The Secret* 2006 DVD www.thesecret.tv and www.drdemartini.com

"When the voice and the vision on the inside become more profound, more clear and loud, than the opinions on the outside, you've mastered your life."

— Dr. John Demartini